Cambridge Elements ≡

Elements in Politics and Society in Latin America
edited by
Maria Victoria Murillo
Columbia University
Juan Pablo Luna
The Pontifical Catholic University of Chile
Tulia G. Falleti
University of Pennsylvania
Andrew Schrank
Brown University

D1329512

DEPENDENCY IN THE TWENTY-FIRST CENTURY?

The Political Economy of China–Latin America Relations

Barbara Stallings

Watson Institute of International and Public Affairs, Brown University

CAMBRIDGE
UNIVERSITY PRESS

CAMBRIDGE
UNIVERSITY PRESS

University Printing House, Cambridge CB2 8BS, United Kingdom

One Liberty Plaza, 20th Floor, New York, NY 10006, USA

477 Williamstown Road, Port Melbourne, VIC 3207, Australia

314–321, 3rd Floor, Plot 3, Splendor Forum, Jasola District Centre,
New Delhi – 110025, India

79 Anson Road, #06–04/06, Singapore 079906

Cambridge University Press is part of the University of Cambridge.

It furthers the University's mission by disseminating knowledge in the pursuit of
education, learning, and research at the highest international levels of excellence.

www.cambridge.org
Information on this title: www.cambridge.org/9781108793032
DOI: 10.1017/9781108875141

First published 2020

A catalogue record for this publication is available from the British Library.

ISBN 978-1-108-79303-2 Paperback
ISSN 2515-5253 (online)
ISSN 2515-5245 (print)

Dependency in the Twenty-First Century?

The Political Economy of China–Latin America Relations

Elements in Politics and Society in Latin America

DOI: 10.1017/9781108875141
First published online: January 2020

Barbara Stallings
Watson Institute of International and Public Affairs, Brown University
Author for correspondence: Barbara Stallings, barbara_stallings@brown.edu

Abstract: The way external forces influence political and economic outcomes in developing countries is an ongoing concern of scholars and policymakers. In the 1970s and 1980s dependency analysis was a popular way of approaching this topic, but it later fell into disrepute. This Element argues that it may be useful to revamp dependency to interpret China's new relationships with developing countries, including those in Latin America. Economic links with China have become important determinants of the region's development. Stallings discusses the dependency debates, reviews the way dependency operated in the US–Latin American case, and analyzes the growing Chinese presence within a dependency framework.

Keywords: Latin America; China; dependency; trade; finance

ISBNs: 9781108793032 (PB), 9781108875141 (OC)
ISSNs: 2515-5253 (online), 2515-5245 (print)

Contents

1 Introduction*

China's relationship with Latin America is a dominant theme in discussions about the region's development prospects in the twenty-first century. A phenomenon that dates mainly from the early 2000s, China's trade with Latin America has increased more than twentyfold since then. In the process, it underpinned economic growth during a decade that came to be known as the China Boom – although that growth has now fallen significantly. In addition, capital flows from China have helped to build transportation links as well as new mining and agricultural projects. Chinese presidents have made ten trips to the region since 2000, while educational and cultural exchanges have burgeoned. At the same time, security links have also increased. The question I address in this Element is how to interpret this new set of relationships.

Evaluation of this evolving partnership has varied substantially. On the positive side, authors have praised the boost to growth, mainly through export-led expansion based on comparative advantage, together with the availability of new sources of capital for investment (Ellis, 2009). At a more detailed level, attention has been called to the particular characteristics of Chinese capital. For example, "patient capital" is said to make it easier for governments to engage in long-term investment projects without having to cut back when bad times hit the region through external shocks (Kaplan, 2016). A related aspect of the China relationship focuses on the greater autonomy for Latin American policymakers, given the diversification of economic ties to include a partner that does not place policy conditions on its money (Wise, 2020). Another contribution is said to be found in the realm of ideas: China's own successful development model is presented as a set of possible lessons for Latin America to follow (Lin and Treichel, 2012).

At the same time, the China–Latin America relationship has aroused concerns about its impact in the region. While the China Boom between 2003 and 2013 featured growth rates reminiscent of the best periods in the postwar era, it was followed by recession as China cut back on its imports. Thus, the old

* I would like to thank participants in three workshops for their comments. At Columbia University in New York: Peter Evans, Tulia Faletti, Robert Kaufman, Vicky Murillo, and Andrew Schrank. At Fudan University in Shanghai: Santiago Bustelo, Peng Hu, Alvaro Méndez, Pippa Morgan, Haibin Niu, Dwayne Woods, Xin Zhang, and Yu Zheng. At the Latin American Faculty of Social Science (FLACSO) in Santiago: Umut Aydin, Angel Flisfisch, Alicia Frohmann, Sebastián Herreros, Juan Pablo Luna, Cecilia Plottier, Carlos Portales, Fernando Reyes Matta, Raúl Sáez, Francisco Urdinez, Alberto van Klaveran, Augusto Varas, and Manfred Wilhelmy. I am also grateful for comments and suggestions from Stephen Kaplan, Atul Kohli, and Carol Wise. Finally, I would like to acknowledge help with data from former colleagues at the United Nations Economic Commission for Latin America and the Caribbean (ECLAC): Laís Abramo, Sebastián Herreros, Keiji Inoue, Xavier Mancero, Cecilia Plottier, Giovanni Stumpo, and Jurgen Weller as well as Margaret Myers of the Inter-American Dialogue.

cyclical pattern of growth reappeared. One reason for the return of stop-go growth was a second source of concern – the so-called reprimarization of Latin America's trade, where the region sells petroleum, metals, and soy to China in return for industrial goods. The price volatility of commodity exports is a well-known cause of growth cycles (Rocha and Bielschowsky, 2018). Given China's high level of competitiveness, because of its low labor costs and subsidized credit, it is hard for Latin American industrial firms to compete (Gallagher and Porzecanski, 2010). Other researchers have pointed to environmental problems deriving from Chinese investments in natural resources (Ray et al., 2017). Inequality in the region, both within and between countries, has also been identified as a consequence of Chinese economic relations with Latin America, whereby South American commodity exporters have benefited compared with Mexico and Central American industrial exporters. Likewise, certain sectors and groups have benefited over others (Gonzalez, 2008).

Beyond evaluating the China–Latin America relationship, much of the new literature has been prescriptive. This has especially been the case with analyses by regional and international organizations (Inter-American Development Bank, 2010, 2014; ECLAC, 2011, 2015, 2016, 2018; World Bank, 2011; OECD/ECLAC/CAF, 2015). Major lessons include the need for Latin American countries to improve education and skills to compete in the twenty-first century world, to promote productivity and innovation, to provide more and better-quality finance, and to devise development strategies vis-à-vis China both at the country and regional levels. Some of the authors cited for their positive views of the China–Latin America relationship have also suggested policy lessons: for example, the need to construct better institutions (Wise, 2020) and to invest borrowed monies more wisely (Kaplan, 2016).

I take a different approach in interpreting the nature of this new relationship. Specifically, I want to explore the utility of a revamped version of dependency analysis to understand China's relations with developing countries in general and Latin America in particular. This goal is perhaps a surprising one since, as discussed in the next section, dependency theory went out of vogue several decades ago. Nonetheless, it has reappeared in a number of articles and books that deal with China and Latin America. Some authors have been highly critical of using dependency (e.g., Wise, 2020). Others have shown more interest in this line of analysis, while also expressing their own concerns (e.g., Jenkins, 2012; Ortiz, 2012; Ferchen et al., 2013; Casanova et al., 2015; Castañeda, 2017).

In this Element, one of several in the Cambridge University Press series "Elements in Politics and Society in Latin America" that will revisit classic concepts that originated in Latin America but spread to other parts of the world, I begin in Section 2 by briefly discussing the origin, spread, and demise of dependency in the twentieth century. I then suggest a way to deal with one of the main criticisms of dependency: the lack of specificity about its mechanisms. This involves three mechanisms – markets, leverage, and linkage – that I argue can help to understand the relationship between external and internal factors in determining the development process. In Section 3, I use these mechanisms to analyze Latin American development under US hegemony after World War II with a focus on the role of dependency in explaining the turn from import-substitution industrialization to the new market-oriented economic model after the debt crisis of the 1980s.

Section 4 moves from the twentieth to the twenty-first century and asks if the same mechanisms can provide a framework for understanding the new relationship between Latin America and the People's Republic of China (PRC). To study the possibility of "dependency with Chinese characteristics," I first compare the United States and China as global and regional hegemons, respectively. I then explore the usefulness of the dependency mechanisms through an analysis of China's relations with Southeast Asia and sub-Saharan Africa, the developing regions that have the longest experience with China. In Sections 5 and 6, I turn to China and Latin America. Section 5 discusses the nature of economic relations (trade and capital flows), while Section 6 focuses on political relations (multilateral and bilateral diplomacy, person-to-person diplomacy, and military and security relations). Section 7 concludes with an evaluation of a dependency framework for analyzing China–Latin America relations as well as some comments on the dependency approach more generally. Overall, my conclusion is that a dependency framework does provide a helpful way to interpret Latin America's important new links with the Asian giant, although flexibility must be used to extend the analysis across centuries and continents.[1]

It is important to underline from the beginning that the short length of this Element means that many important details and nuances cannot be explored. In particular, much of the discussion is carried on at the level of regions – Latin America as well as Southeast Asia and sub-Saharan Africa. Of course, averages at the regional, or even the country, level can be misleading simplifications. While I try to point this out where it is especially relevant, a true understanding of the processes studied here would require much more detailed case study analysis. My hope is that this Element will stimulate such work.

---

[1] Two recent books that are complementary to this one, in that they look at the China–Latin America relationship in comparative perspective, are Jenkins (2019) on Africa and Latin America and an edited collection by Eisenman and Heginbotham (2018) that analyzes China's relations with many developing regions.

2 A Brief Reprise on Dependency

In the early 1960s, two approaches to explaining development dominated academic and policy discussion. One was so-called modernization theory; the other was the Solow model within neoclassical economics. The two were similar in a couple of ways: both defined development as the characteristics embodied in then "developed" countries, and both saw the process of development as one of convergence. The main differences were methodological. Modernization theory was interdisciplinary, while the Solow model was the purview of economists. Modernization theory, which had two variants, economic and cultural, portrayed development as occurring in stages from primitive societies to ones based on "high mass consumption." The main drivers were shifts in economic and cultural factors internal to the societies themselves. The Solow model predicted a convergence between developed and developing countries, since the latter were expected to grow more rapidly.[2]

2.1 The Origins of Dependency

In Latin America, experts and policymakers became increasingly critical of both approaches. These critics can be divided into two groups. One came out of a structuralist tradition, based at the United Nations (UN) Economic Commission for Latin America (ECLA) in Santiago, Chile; the other was manifested intellectually as a Latin American version of Marxism. By the late 1960s, both of these currents had begun to advocate the concept of "dependency" to explain why convergence could not be expected between developed and developing countries in the twentieth century.

The version of dependency coming out of Marxism was mainly associated with the writings of Andre Gunder Frank, a German economist based in Santiago, Chile.[3] Frank argued that from the sixteenth century on, the region had been part of an open, export-oriented, capitalist economy, dominated by European and later US monopolies. This situation led to the expropriation of the economic surplus of Latin America and the polarization of the international economy into "a metropolitan center and peripheral satellites" (1967: 8). Moreover, he argued that "national capitalism and the national bourgeoisie do not and cannot offer any way out of underdevelopment in Latin America" (1967: xv), so the only way for development to occur was via a socialist

---

[2] The classic work behind economic modernization was Rostow (1960). On the cultural side, a number of authors were important; see Valenzuela and Valenzuela (1978) for citations. The Solow model was produced virtually simultaneously by Solow (1956) and Swan (1956).

[3] Frank's best-known work (1967) was published in English by Monthly Review Press. In addition to Frank, a number of Latin American social scientists were writing in a similar vein. See, for example, dos Santos (1968), Marini (1972), and Caputo and Pizarro (1974).

revolution. Whether Frank intended it or not, the dependency analysis with which he was identified stressed forces from outside a developing country, leaving little space for agency on the part of domestic actors. Thus, it became an easy target for critics.

A more subtle and complex version of dependency theory, associated with structuralism, was the work of a Brazilian sociologist, Fernando Henrique Cardoso, and a Chilean historian, Enzo Faletto, both of whom worked at ECLA.[4] Not surprisingly, they joined others at ECLA who advocated more emphasis on social and political analysis, not just on economics. Like many colleagues, they saw themselves as using both structural and historical tools. While they began with the assumption that the development of Latin America had been and was still conditioned by the international capitalist system, they were especially interested in exploring the impact of external actors and markets on internal politics and society. A particular concern was the formation of coalitions that might link international and domestic actors.

Their work differed in two main ways from that of Frank. On the one hand, they were not interested in a grand theory of development or even the development of Latin America, but in the analysis of "concrete situations of dependency." In the phase of classical dependency, the main situations were defined according to whether the principal export firms were owned by local or foreign capital, which had various impacts on development. On the other hand, the authors were much more positive than Frank about the possibilities for at least some countries to arrive at a capitalist style of development, which the authors labeled associated dependent development or simply dependent development.[5] Dependent development was another situation of dependency.

Dependent development involved industrialization, based on consumer goods that were widely available in the North but luxuries in developing countries. The distinction meant that industrialization sharpened income inequality and structural heterogeneity in Latin America. As a consequence, Cardoso and Faletto said they were making a double criticism. "We criticize those who expect permanent stagnation in underdeveloped dependent countries … But we also criticize those who expect capitalistic development of peripheral economies to solve problems

---

[4] The main Cardoso–Faletto work was first published in Spanish in 1969 by Siglo XXI (Cardoso and Faletto, 1969). It was not translated into English until 1979, so many thought it was a later reaction to the Frank book. In actuality, all were writing at the same time in Santiago, although there is no evidence of significant interaction among them. It is important to note that Cardoso and Faletto claimed an eclectic intellectual heritage, despite the common view that their analysis relied heavily on ECLA's brand of structuralism.

[5] The term "dependent development" was popularized by Evans (1979) in his analysis of Brazil under that title.

such as distribution of property, full employment, better income distribution, and better living conditions for people" (1979: xxiii–xxiv).[6]

Complementing dependency analysis — and, some would say, going beyond it – was world system theory, introduced by Immanuel Wallerstein (1974). Coming out of the study of Africa rather than Latin America, Wallerstein stressed the unity of a single world capitalist system and its historical origins. In addition, he made the center-periphery dichotomy more nuanced by introducing the concept of the semi-periphery, which constitutes a source of stability in the world system (Wallerstein, 1976). The semi-periphery bears some resemblance to dependent development in the Cardoso–Faletto schema. Another of Wallerstein's contributions, which is useful for my analysis, was the idea that while the system persists, individual countries – including hegemons – can change their positions. Interestingly, world systems theory has proved more long-lived than dependency, enjoying several institutional bases and an ever-growing list of publications.

2.2 The Spread of Dependency

The dependency approach was extremely influential in the analysis of development (or lack thereof) in Latin America in the 1970s and 1980s, displacing both modernization and neoclassical economics. Moreover, dependency analysis was adopted and adapted by other developing regions, including sub-Saharan Africa, South Asia, and, more recently, Eastern Europe. In East Asia, however, dependency hit a wall. The dominant theory in that region argued that the "developmental state" was the most important determinant of East Asia's extremely high growth rates (Haggard, 2018).

The area that showed most interest in dependency was sub-Saharan Africa, following independence in the majority of countries in the 1960s. Because of their recent emergence from colonial status, the term "neocolonialism" was also used with great frequency, but it embodied many of the same characteristics as dependency. Two prominent African specialists (Apter and Rosberg, 1994: 32) said that dependency analysis "had an enormous impact on the shape of African studies." Leys (1975), the author of an influential book on post-independence Kenya, put it this way: "it was necessary to realize that the relationship between the 'private sector' and the pattern of post-independence development could not be understood in purely Kenyan terms, but was the outcome of international forces" (p. ix). He added: "A theoretical framework, which does address itself

---

[6] In the preface to the English translation of their book, Cardoso and Faletto argued that socialism was necessary for a more positive version of development. This was not the message of the original Spanish version. Moreover, when Cardoso became president of Brazil, he followed a very different path; see also Cardoso (2009).

directly to the questions with which this study is concerned, is to be found in the work of 'underdevelopment' and 'dependency' theorists" (pp. xii–xiii).[7]

In South Asia, the dependency framework had a mixed reception. Thus, Kohli (2004) argued that the powerful alliance of Indian nationalists and businessmen, via a strong state, was key to the development of the largest country in South Asia. He said that "the case of India's nearly autarkic but sluggish industrialization could be construed as a heavy indictment of the dependency proposition … although the absence of foreign capital and technology contributed to an inefficient and slow pattern of industrial growth in India" (p. 380). If India was large enough to go its own way, especially given the ideology of its founding leaders, this was not necessarily the case for the smaller countries in the region. Dependency theory was used by a number of analysts looking at Pakistan and Bangladesh, especially on topics such as foreign aid and foreign debt.[8]

Even experts on Eastern Europe, which was sometimes referred to before 1989 as an example of socialist dependency,[9] have found relevance for dependency analysis in explaining trends in the broader European context today. For example, Bruszt and Vukov (2018), in the introduction to a set of papers on the integration of Eastern and Southern European countries into the European Union, argued for the use of a center-periphery framework. "Drawing on the long tradition in the political economy of development, we argue that integration among countries at different levels of economic competitiveness may create specific vulnerabilities for the peripheral states" (p. 154).

In East Asia, however, dependency did not seem to fit – although some of the most prominent critics appeared to have had Frank's version of dependency in mind rather than the more sophisticated work of Cardoso and Faletto. For example, Amsden (1979) held that the case of Taiwan refuted dependency analysis because internal factors were more important than external ones. Haggard (1990), who was more familiar with the Latin American debates,

---

[7] Although Leys himself later changed his mind about dependency, many others used the framework. See, for example, Brett (1971), Amin (1972), McGowan (1976), Zartman (1976), Vengroff (1977), Higgott (1980), Carlsson (1983), Okolo (1983), Bienefeld (1988), Yates (1996), Moss et al. (2005), and Kindiki (2014). Some of these are general works, others are country case studies; some see dependency as useful, others are more critical. For an early comparison of dependency in Africa and Latin America, see Stallings (1972). Two studies that use a dependency perspective to analyze Africa's relations with China are Taylor (2014) and Agbebi and Virtanen (2017).

[8] See, for example, Chaudhary (1988) and Kahn and Asghar (2015) on Pakistan; Sobhan (1996), Bhattacharya (2007), and Hassan (2011) on Bangladesh. McCartney (2011) specifically calls attention to the different response to the dependency approach in the smaller South Asian countries compared to India.

[9] See discussion in Packenham (1982) on socialist dependency. He uses the case of Cuba, but many of the same arguments would hold for Eastern Europe.

argued that dependency analysis suffered from the same weakness as neoclassical economics in trying to analyze East Asia: both neglected politics and institutions.

Despite such critiques, there were experts on East Asia who were more positive. In an analysis of the auto industry in three Southeast Asian countries, for example, Abbott (2003: 154) criticized dependency theory for focusing on broad generalizations, while also declaring that "dependency remains a useful and necessary conceptual tool of economic analysis at a sub-generalized, sectoral-specific level despite the theoretical inadequacies and flaws of generalized theories of dependency." In addition, several authors who wrote about dependency in Latin America argued in favor of its utility in the East Asian context. For instance, Gereffi (1989) pointed out that the characteristics of dependent development were different in the two regions: dependency in East Asia had been a product of a heavy reliance on foreign aid and trade, while dependency in Latin America was based on extensive involvement with transnational corporations and banks. These different configurations, he argued, would not be expected to produce similar outcomes.

2.3 The Demise of Dependency

Despite the popularity of dependency analysis in the 1970s and 1980s, the concept fell into disrepute by the 1990s and was rarely used from then on. Criticisms came from many directions, and the debates were confused by the multiplicity of approaches that were joined under the label of dependency. Four main intellectual criticisms can be identified; in addition, certain trends in the world also contributed to the demise of dependency analysis.

A first criticism, voiced by many if not most critics of dependency, was its lack of specificity, its global scope – its general "fuzziness." How was dependency to be defined? Through what mechanisms did it operate? What were its effects? In particular, what was its relationship to development? Did dependency operate in the same way everywhere? Did it change over time and, if so, how? What was the opposite of dependency? How could the theory be falsified? These questions reflected frustration with a concept that was used in many different ways. Scholars and policymakers were talking past each other, in part because of disagreement on the role that dependency analysis was meant to play in approaches to development. Of course, there were also differences in the definition of development, and an overlap often existed in the way the two terms were used.

A second criticism followed from the first. What was the epistemological status of dependency, and what methodology should be used to study it? With respect to the former, the main issue was whether dependency constituted a theory or simply a framework or approach.[10] If dependency was a theory, then hypotheses could be derived and tested.[11] This tendency was part of a more general shift in the social sciences from grand to middle-range theory that could be tested, often by quantitative methods. Such scholarship was fiercely combated by some adherents of dependency. Cardoso himself (1977) published an article on "The Consumption of Dependency Theory in the United States," in which he said:

> I do not agree with the idea that to improve the quality of analysis, the theory of dependency should be formalized so that, after testing hypotheses derived from this formalization, one could venture out into the world waving the banner of the percentage of variation explained by each factor ... [I]t would be better to ask for an improvement in the quality of historical-structural analysis (p. 21).

A third set of critiques concerned an alleged overemphasis on international relationships and corresponding neglect of domestic forces. The Marxist left, especially among Latin Americans and Latin Americanists, argued that dependency analysis did not pay sufficient attention to social classes and class struggle.[12] Experts on East Asia denounced dependency for not recognizing that the state was more important than foreign capital in determining development possibilities. One version of this argument said that dependency analysts had mixed up causality: foreign capital did not determine development strategies; rather, development strategies determined the need (or not) for foreign capital. If the state – generally defined in this literature as government bureaucrats – made the proper decisions, it could control foreign capital (Haggard, 1986).

The success of the Asian economies also gave rise to a fourth criticism of dependency analysis. A growing body of experts argued that external flows (capital, trade, technology, and ideas) had a *positive* impact on development. The proof usually offered was the East Asian economies, which were not only growing faster, but had more equal distributions of income and were able to recover more rapidly from the shocks of the 1970s and early 1980s than had the less open economies of Latin America or Africa. A more moderate version of this critique was not as positive about the benefits of openness, and indeed

---

[10] A discussion of the theoretical status of the dependency literature is offered in Palma (1978).

[11] A number of US scholars were interested in trying to develop quantitative criteria to measure dependency and to use those measures to test hypotheses about the impact of dependency on development. See, for example, Kaufman et al. (1975), Duvall (1978), McGowan and Smith (1978), and Jackman (1982).

[12] Examples of this type of criticism are contained in Chilcote (1982) and Munck (1984).

pointed out that the East Asian economies were not uniformly open to imports or direct investment, but insisted that explanations must be provided for the great differences in economic performance among developing countries given that all faced similar external conditions.[13]

Beyond intellectual and policy critiques, political and economic events occurring in the world helped to undermine the influence of dependency analysis. One was the enormous quantity of loans available to developing countries during the 1970s. These loans relieved foreign exchange constraints and increased the power of governments vis-à-vis multinational corporations (MNCs), which had been seen as the most important agents of dependency.[14] Second, an intellectual consensus began to crystalize among leaders of the industrial countries and the international financial institutions (IFIs) about the benefits of open trade regimes and smaller governments. As the 1970s loan binge came to an end in the early 1980s, the power behind this consensus began to grow as the IFIs – rather than private bankers – controlled the available capital (Kahler, 1990). A final blow was the fall of socialism in the Soviet Union and Eastern Europe. Marxism, an important underpinning for dependency analysis, fell into disrepute as a consequence. Equally telling, the main examples of noncapitalist development disappeared as did Soviet financial support for developing country governments that opposed orthodox policies.[15]

The combination of intellectual critiques and international trends that reinforced them had a devastating effect on dependency analysis: it was rarely mentioned by the 1990s. At the same time, the issues dealt with by dependency analysts did not go away. Indeed, they became more serious in the 1990s and beyond, as Latin American and other developing economies became more open and thus more vulnerable to damaging external shocks. Also, as I will discuss in later sections, dependency analysis may provide a useful framework for thinking about the new relationship between China and developing countries.

2.4 Mechanisms of Dependency and Definitions

In discussions of dependency during the 1970s and 1980s, the main economic mechanisms were trade relations and international investment (foreign direct investment or FDI, bond issues, and loans). Accompanying these economic mechanisms were political relations between dominant and dependent

---

[13] A comparative analysis of the external shocks in developing countries is given in Belassa and McCarthy (1984). A version of this analysis also came from the Marxist left; see Warren (1980). On the East Asian case, see Haggard (1986).

[14] On the use of loans to escape from direct investment, see Frieden (1981).

[15] On the implications of the changes in Eastern Europe and the Soviet Union for socialist ideology, see Przeworski (1990).

countries, including military and diplomatic relations as well as an affinity between financial and other elites across the North–South divide. Later, in the postwar period, multilateral institutions became part of the web of political actors, and "soft power" would become more important as time went on. In an earlier essay (Stallings, 1992), I combined these mechanisms into three groups: markets, leverage, and linkage. I finish this section with a discussion of the three and definitions of dependency and development that will be used later in this Element.

2.4.1 Markets

Markets represent the economic context within which developing countries operate. The two major external markets relevant to the development process are for exports and finance. In the heyday of dependency, the principal international markets for developing country exports were in the industrial countries. Demand for exports is a function of the growth rates and the level of protection in importing countries. With a few important exceptions, developing countries are price takers, so terms-of-trade shifts are determined exogenously. When the volume of exports declines or negative price shifts occur, severe economic problems can result. If finance is not available to cover trade deficits, imports must be cut, leading to lower consumption and/or investment.

The importance of financial markets is related to the trade balance but also to past borrowing patterns, since new borrowing may be required to service old debts. Like terms of trade, terms of borrowing – interest, fees, maturity – are largely determined exogenously. These terms vary by type of lender, with public lenders generally having softer terms than their private counterparts. During the era preceding the 1980s debt crisis, which will play an important role in the next section, private banks tended to lend at floating interest rates that shifted much of the risk to borrowers.

While short-term fluctuations and long-term trends in international markets are important for all countries, evidence indicates that developing countries are particularly vulnerable to negative shocks (Barrot, Calderón, and Servén, 2016). Likewise, booms and busts will have differential impacts, depending on the factor endowment and economic structure of individual countries. With respect to trade shocks, a country with an open economy will be in special jeopardy. The structure of exports and imports is also crucial. Raw materials are particularly susceptible to price shocks, while industrial exports can face a challenge through protection. Diversification provides shelter from trade shocks, but developing countries tend to be less diversified. A second set of characteristics – usually found in developing countries – further increases susceptibility to financial shocks: a low volume of export revenue and/or low domestic savings increases vulnerability to a cutoff of finance or a sharp rise in its price.

These shocks also have important political implications. In extreme cases, governments can fall as a result of severe economic difficulties. There has been extensive debate on the relationship between economic crisis and democracy,[16] although authoritarian governments can also fall as a result of economic crises. During expansive periods, governments can reward supporters through increasing wages and social services, which makes coalition building relatively easy. Under these conditions, distribution can be accomplished without *re*distribution. In contractive periods, in contrast, not only are resources unavailable for social services or employment in government agencies, but some kinds of political-economic strategies become nonviable. Thus, populism is found more often in boom periods.

2.4.2 Leverage

Powerful actors will always seek to influence outcomes of market processes. Leverage, by contrast, involves mechanisms whereby economic or political actors specifically set out to influence the behavior of others – usually those who are less powerful. It involves the direct use of power, with a promise of a reward (or a threat of punishment) for carrying out (or not) a desired action.

The most obvious kind of leverage is one country's use of its military to force another to behave in a certain way. This tactic is used less frequently than in past centuries, but it still occurs. In the postwar period, the United States invaded a number of Latin American countries that were perceived as supporting "socialism" or "communism." Prominent examples included Guatemala (1954), the Dominican Republic (1965), Grenada (1983), and Panama (1989). In other parts of the world, there have been many cases of such intervention, including in recent years.

More common than overt military force, but more difficult to document, is the use of covert intelligence operations to get governments to change their policies. Covert actions are especially effective if carried out in conjunction with local actors in the target country. Many of the examples of covert operations that we are aware of involve unsuccessful activities. CIA training for an invasion of Cuba in the Bay of Pigs (1960) is such an example, as is the Nicaraguan "contra" operation in the 1980s. CIA operations during the Allende government (1970–3) in Chile came to light through congressional hearings in the United States.

---

[16] For a recent analysis, see Campello (2015); an older contribution is Remmer (1990). A comparison of the 1930s and 1980s is found in Drake (1989).

Economic forms of leverage are the most frequently used today. They can involve providing access (or not) to markets, where bilateral or plurilateral free trade agreements (FTAs) have become an important tool. More common is leverage involving access to finance. Financial leverage is most effective when resources are scarce, creditors are unified, and the incentives they offer are credible. The best-known kind of economic leverage in the postwar period has involved conditionality bargains with IFIs, especially the International Monetary Fund (IMF) and the World Bank. The types of economic policies required to obtain finance from the IFIs range from simple demand management policies for an IMF standby loan through extensive structural reforms and opening to foreign capital for a World Bank structural adjustment loan. Bilateral aid agencies have also been frequent users of conditionality, but often of a more political sort. The use of sanctions is relevant here.

Private actors vary in their interest in, and ability to exert, financial leverage. For example, private banks in the 1970s disbursed large numbers of loans with very few strings attached; they had neither the will nor capacity to impose conditions. When the debt crisis broke out in 1982, however, the situation rapidly changed. The banks joined forces with the IFIs and industrial country governments to reschedule loans in exchange for orthodox economic policies and the continuation of debt-service payments. Today, bondholders are the main source of financial leverage, but their capacity to exert leverage over borrowers depends on their ability to coordinate activities among holders of individual bond issues. MNCs were the major external actors in dependency analysis. They were accused of displacing local firms and workers, coercing governments into providing lucrative investment incentives, and shifting decision-making to their headquarters in the North. In the current period, public opinion toward MNCs has changed dramatically. As developing countries have become more interested in exporting, MNCs are seen more favorably as powerful allies in the quest to gain access to markets, technology, and financing – although concerns remain about asymmetrical power relations.

The scope for economic leverage has thus varied over time and with country characteristics. For example, a large domestic market and valuable natural resource endowments can give a host country substantial power. Another important characteristic is state capacity, which is relevant in at least two ways. On the one hand, a high level of state capacity is necessary to negotiate effectively with private investors. On the other hand, in dealing with IFIs, the ability to design alternative types of economic programs is crucial.

2.4.3 Linkage

Linkage is the set of relationships – based on ideas, education, employment, living experience – whereby actors in dependent countries come to identify their interests with those of a more powerful country.[17] The concept of linkage was particularly stressed in the Cardoso–Faletto (1979) analysis of dependency. Thus, they said: "[T]here is no metaphysical relation of dependence between one nation and another, between one state and another. These relations are made possible through a network of interests ... that bind some social groups to others, some classes to others" (p. 173).

Businesspeople constitute the most important network for economic policy-making. Two categories have been suggested to differentiate business groups: exporters versus those producing for the domestic market, whereby the former are more likely to have international ties. These ties involve both interests (access to markets, technology, and finance) and culture (education, travel, and consumption patterns). Top-level technocrats are also likely to have studied abroad, which results in a double kind of identification with a dominant country. Most obvious is the professional knowledge transmitted within the preferred paradigms of the industrial countries, which can be further reinforced through cultural ties. Moreover, many developing-country technocrats spend time working in the IFIs, which furthers their identification with the policies espoused by these institutions. Military technocrats and leaders from developing countries constitute another group likely to have received training abroad. The US military has traditionally set up training programs for top military brass in developing countries. This training is supplemented by the purchase of US equipment.

The middle class is a much more diffuse component of the network of interests that Cardoso and Faletto spoke of. Middle-class groups are linked mainly though consumption and lifestyle ambitions. Through the media, imported products become known and the perceived necessity to purchase them provides a powerful link with counterparts in industrial countries. For the upper middle class, ownership of goods is supplemented by travel and perhaps education abroad. In situations like that of Latin America, where the majority of the population considers itself middle class, the significance for political support building is obvious.

When ruling political coalitions are closely tied to internationally oriented groups, they are likely to have different policy orientations than governments where labor, marginal urban residents, and domestically oriented businesses

---

[17] Nye's (2004) concept of soft power is closely related to linkage from the point of view of the more powerful countries.

constitute the pillars of government support. Most importantly, winners and losers will vary. Coalitions can come to power in various ways related to these networks of interest. In a democracy, coalitions must seek broad support, which is likely to rely on appeals to the middle class. Once an internationally oriented coalition is in power, by whatever means, the orientation of technocrats becomes important.

The effectiveness of international linkage networks is likely to vary according to two factors discussed previously. One relates to economic structure. The more open the economy, the more reliant it is on international trade and finance, the more dense will be the international networks. A second factor has to do with the state of international markets. In times of global economic crisis, the influence of technocrats is likely to increase in any kind of government. Likewise, a crisis can give an edge to a coalition that claims to have access to foreign assets.

2.4.4 Interactions among Dependency Mechanisms

While the dependency mechanisms were presented as three separate concepts, a good deal of overlap exists among them. In ideal textbook terms, markets operate on their own without interference from governments or interest groups. In this sense, they simply provide a context in which economic and political actions take place. For example, in a boom period, it is easy for governments or private actors to obtain access to finance to carry out desired projects. Likewise, it is easier to form political coalitions when resources are flowing freely. In the real world, however, markets are generally manipulated in one way or other, so they can serve as tools of leverage. Indeed, it may be useful to think of economic versus political leverage, where the former relies on providing or restricting access to economic assets and the latter relies on use of political threats or actual force.

Both types of leverage involve power relations, but work best when combined with linkage. If leverage implies the use of some kind of force by a more powerful actor to achieve a desired end, linkage is less costly since it leads the world-be targets of leverage to *want* to behave as the more powerful actor wishes. Important cases, as already seen, include local business people, technocrats, and military officers who identify with external actors. To provide an economic example of leverage and linkage, it is clearly better to have a local finance minister follow policies to maintain debt payments to an international bank because she thinks it is right, rather than to have the IMF threaten to cut off funds if payments are not made. In a more extreme political example, if a foreign military is involved in a coup in a developing country, it surely prefers to have the collaboration of local armed forces rather than occupy the country.

In the following sections of the Element, we will see how the relative importance of the three mechanisms, their particular characteristics, and the interactions among them vary according to "situations of dependency" in Cardoso and Faletto's term. Those situations are the joint outcome of external and internal actors and forces, including the characteristics of the hegemonic power(s) in the world system at a given time.

2.4.5 Definitions

Before embarking on a study of potential dependency relations in the US–Latin American context in the late twentieth century or the Chinese–Latin American context in the early twenty-first century, we need definitions of both dependency and development. Here, I rely on definitions that are consistent with the usage in the Cardoso–Faletto analysis, since that is the approach to dependency used in this Element.

In the preface of the English-language version of their book, Cardoso and Faletto write, "[f]rom the economic point of view a system is dependent when the accumulation and expansion of capital cannot find its essential dynamic inside the system" (1979: xx). They go on to mention three capabilities neces- sary for escaping dependency: the creation of new technologies, the production of capital goods, and a solid banking system to provide finance. Of develop- ment, they say: "[Dependent] development ... means the progress of productive forces, mainly through the import of technology, capital accumulation, penetra- tion of local economies by foreign enterprises, increasing numbers of wage- earning groups, and intensification of the social division of labor" (1979: xxiv). In their analysis, and in that of most other dependency analysts, a proxy for development is GDP growth and especially industrialization. While a focus on the welfare of the majority of the population is an alternative definition, Cardoso and Faletto go on to say that dependent development will not resolve problems of equity and wellbeing for the majority. In the empirical section throughout the Element, I will look both at growth and its sectoral allocation and at who benefits. This combination provides a more complete understanding of the development process and the (possible) impact of dependency.

3 Dependency in Latin America under US Hegemony

As World War II ended, the United States replaced Britain as the dominant political and economic power in the world. Since the US economy was stronger than any other and the military had been beefed up during the war, the United States abandoned the reluctance it had shown during the interwar period to assume hegemonic status. The immediate concern was to rebuild Europe and later Japan and to establish an institutional framework for the postwar era. The latter included the creation of the UN, the IMF, the World Bank, and the General Agreement on Tariffs and Trade, together with a number of regional development banks and UN commissions.

Latin America was initially of little concern for the new hegemon, although of course the United States had not been completely absent from the region previously. The Monroe Doctrine proclaimed future US ambitions with respect to its southern neighbors as early as 1823. Later, participation in the so-called Spanish–American War in 1898 gave the United States quasi-colonies in Puerto Rico and the Philippines as well as major influence over Cuba. Moreover, US capital had begun to flow to the region by the end of the nineteenth century, accompanied by various demonstrations of military power to ensure that debts were paid through the policy known as dollar diplomacy (Stallings, 1987).

Throughout the following century, the United States played a dominant role in the political and economic processes and outcomes in the region, as will be documented later in this section of the Element. I argue that the resulting set of interactions is well captured through a dependency framework. I concentrate on the postwar period and divide it into the years before and after the debt crisis of the 1980s and the change in development model that accompanied the crisis. In the earlier period, under a relatively closed economy guided by the state, the economic mechanisms of dependency held less sway than they would later. Nonetheless, the operation of markets helped shape economic trends, while overt and covert political actions undermined those governments that sought to control external forces. The combined roles of markets and economic leverage helped to bring about the change in model toward one with a more open economy and a greater role for the private sector, which was influenced by linkages with international counterparts. In the more open context, markets gained influence and external actors worked together with domestic actors to promote policies that increased growth and made them the main beneficiaries.

3.1 Import Substitution Industrialization

Latin America entered the new world order in 1945 with a legacy from three centuries of colonial rule, but more importantly a century of domination by Britain. Regional economies were heavily reliant on a small number of natural resource exports, and their fiscal expenditures and investment depended on capital from abroad. The nascent industrial sector that existed in some countries required imported equipment and inputs and could not compete with foreign products without the help of high tariffs. Multiple defaults during the previous century had tarnished the region's reputation in the bond markets, so MNCs were destined to play a crucial role in finance. In the social sphere, education levels were quite low, and inequality was high and increasing.

When the war ended, Latin American governments were eager to turn to promoting development. Debates focused on which policies to follow and how to finance the large-scale investments that would be required. The import substitution industrialization (ISI) period can be dated from the publication in 1950 of a diagnosis of Latin American economies by Raúl Prebisch, executive secretary of ECLA. The basic argument was that productivity gains generated in the industrial sector of the core countries were captured through higher wages, rather than resulting in lower prices; productivity was lower in primary production in the periphery with wages held down by surplus labor. A second – and better known, but highly controversial – argument concerned the alleged deteriorating terms of trade for primary products compared to industrial goods, which was said to be the result of higher income elasticity of demand for the latter. Based on this analysis, ECLA proposed that Latin America should push to industrialize. Industrialization, in turn, would require that governments take a more active role in the economy, but foreign capital would also have to be a partner in the provision of finance and technology.[18]

Regional responses to ECLA's proposals varied by the size and strength of the industrial sector in different countries in the early 1950s. Six of them – Argentina, Brazil, Chile, Colombia, Mexico, and Uruguay – had already achieved substantial industrialization in the late nineteenth century, which expanded as a result of import restrictions during World War II. Indeed, these countries had virtually completed what would come to be called the easy phase of ISI (the production of basic consumer goods). Because of the damage caused by external shocks during the Great Depression of the 1930s, the six were eager to abandon export-led growth. The remainder of the region, including most of the smaller economies, was less industrialized and not as eager to adopt the ISI proposals. The continuation of export-led growth based on raw materials appeared to them to be an easier option.

The countries that wanted to strengthen and expand their industrial sectors began to undertake policy changes that they hoped would advance this process. Tariffs on imports were one of the most important policy tools. While tariffs had been in place previously for revenue purposes, the idea was to use them in a more strategic way to protect new industries that would be established. Another crucial policy involved finance for the investments in new industries or the expansion of existing ones. Given the lack of local capital markets and limited

---

[18] The original document is ECLA (1950). The best sources on ECLA's philosophy and policy recommendations are two edited volumes by Bielschowsky (1998, 2010).

access to international bond markets, governments revised legislation to attract MNCs.

Five of the six countries achieved substantial success in expanding industry in the 1950s and 1960s.[19] GDP growth averaged 5.3 percent annually between 1945 and 1973, and manufacturing was the engine of that growth (Thorp, 1998: chp. 6). Since they had already made major inroads into the local production of basic consumer goods, the next step was to begin production of consumer durables and eventually intermediate and capital goods. Of course, these types of goods required more capital and a higher level of technology than basic consumer goods, so foreign capital became even more important. Some governments were reluctant to rely on foreign corporations (Bulmer-Thomas, 2014: 301), but there did not seem to be an alternative.

Thus, MNCs, mainly from the United States, were invited to Latin America for their technology, marketing, management skills, and financial resources. Soon, however, differences in approach began to manifest themselves. While Latin American governments hoped the MNCs would produce capital and intermediate goods and export manufactured products, the interest of the corporations was to sell consumer goods in the protected markets of the largest countries. Probably exporting manufactured goods would have been difficult in any case because of the high unit costs of firms that had small production runs and were protected from competition. Other conflicts arose over the use of transfer pricing to avoid taxes and the sourcing of investment capital on local markets. Controversy also appeared over governments' desires to have a high level of inputs produced locally and their objections to the transfer of resources out of the countries when profits and interest payments exceeded capital inflows.

In addition to frictions with foreign investors, other problems emerged in the ISI process. Most important were balance-of-payments deficits, given that the MNCs were mainly selling in the domestic markets. They were also importing inputs and capital goods, just as local firms had done previously. Countries continued to rely on primary-product exports, but the incoming revenues were insufficient and the prices highly volatile. ECLA economists decided that the problem was the small size of the domestic markets in Latin America. Their solution was regional integration, which was inspired by the formation of the European Economic Community in 1958.

During the 1960s several regional integration groups were formed. The first was the Latin American Free Trade Area (LAFTA) in 1960, composed of all of the main South American countries plus Mexico. At the end of 1960, the Central American Common Market (CACM) came into being. It was followed nearly a

---

[19] Uruguay fell behind because its domestic market was too small to support ISI.

decade later by the Andean Pact in 1969, consisting of Bolivia, Chile, Colombia, Ecuador, Peru, and Venezuela. All of these groups suffered splits and reorganizations.[20] The bottom line, however, was that regional integration did not solve the problems encountered by ISI. Members were not willing to give up sovereignty, nor were they willing to accept the division of product lines necessary to obtain the advantages of a larger regionalized market.

While not all countries were able to ride the ISI strategy to success, several developed very sophisticated manufacturing capacity. Thus Brazil and Mexico were typically cast together with South Korea and Taiwan as "newly industrializing economies." Evans' (1979) analysis of Brazil as a case of dependent development is the best example both of the success of the ISI development strategy as well as its shortcomings. In explaining Brazil's impressive level of industrialization, Evans portrayed MNCs as the "main character" in the story. But this protagonist combined forces with a strong state and a national bourgeoisie to form a "triple alliance." The alliance, in turn, was able to increase capital accumulation and improve technological capacity to lift Brazil from the periphery into the semi-periphery. Nonetheless, it was "inherently incapable of serving the needs of the mass of the population" (p. 13).

Many changes in economic and political relations came about during the 1970s in the international environment as well as Latin America itself. A number of developing countries, including some in Latin America, had come to believe that they were not fully benefiting from international growth, trade, and capital flows. Indeed, this was the heyday of dependency analysis. Nationalism was on the rise in many parts of the world. It included the inauguration of numerous governments that wanted to limit the power of privileged groups, both domestic and foreign, and to give more power and economic benefits to "the masses." Some called themselves socialist; others did not. In either case, the US response was often intervention, overt or covert, to overthrow the governments and restore the status quo ante. Cases of US interference in the 1960s included Haiti, Guatemala, Ecuador, Brazil, Peru, and the Dominican Republic; in the 1970s, in addition to the well-known case of Chile, there were also Bolivia, Costa Rica, Jamaica, and Nicaragua at the end of the decade.[21]

A key turning point was the quadrupling of oil prices in late 1973 by the Organization of Petroleum Exporting Countries (OPEC). The oil shock sent the world economy into a tailspin. Since most Latin American countries were oil

---

[20] What are currently the most important regional organizations – Mercosur and the Pacific Alliance – came later. For a useful account of the regional integration process, see Baumann (2008).

[21] On these cases and others, see Blum (1995), Kinzer (2006), and McPherson (2016).

importers, the result was to exacerbate their balance-of-payments problems and thus threaten their economies. The region's few oil exporters, of course, experienced a very different situation.[22] As it happened, the oil shock itself provided an apparent solution for oil importers. The OPEC countries deposited their sudden cache of resources in the major international banks, which had to lend out the money to pay interest to the depositors.

Eager bankers met eager borrowers in Latin America and other oil importing countries. Not since the 1920s had there been such a frenzy of foreign loans – although the mechanism shifted from bond issues to loans from large commercial banks (Stallings, 1987). By the end of the 1970s, Latin America had accumulated an enormous debt with the international private banks. Between 1960 and 1982, total external debt of Latin America increased from US$7 billion to US$314 billion. The share of the debt owed to private banks went from 16 percent to 58 percent, and debt service rose from 18 percent of exports to 50 percent (Bulmer-Thomas, 2014: table 10.5).

3.2 The Debt Crisis and the New Economic Model

This debt proved impossible to service, given Latin America's limited export revenues and spiking international interest rates. In August 1982, Mexico declared that it would be forced to default if it did not receive international financial support. The ensuing years saw a highly asymmetrical battle erupt between debtor countries and creditor banks. A few Latin American governments tried to form a debtors' cartel, but their differing interests (and side payments from lenders) made it impossible. The banks, by contrast, did act in concert through bankers' committees for each country, supported by the banks' home governments and the IFIs. Before the banks eventually agreed to write off some of the debt through the plan introduced by US treasury secretary, Nicolas Brady, Latin American countries had been forced to follow austerity policies that led to a "lost decade" – when per capita growth during the 1980s was nil.[23]

The impact of the debt crisis was not only low growth, but increased poverty rates and social ills. The crisis also marked the end of the closed-economy industrialization policies that Latin America had been following in the postwar period. They were replaced by a new economic model, which was varyingly labelled neoliberalism, the Washington Consensus, or simply a market-oriented development strategy. While many analysts portrayed the new model as being imposed on Latin America as a

---

[22] Venezuela, Latin America's largest oil exporter, was among the five original members of OPEC.

[23] There is an enormous literature on the Latin American debt crisis. Among others, see Cline (1984, 1995), Griffith Jones (1988), and Devlin (1989). A banker's perspective is Rhodes (2011). A recent historical perspective is Ocampo et al. (2014).

consequence of the debt crisis, the process behind the adoption of these policies was actually more complex. Certainly, outside pressure existed, but many Latin American policymakers, especially those trained in the United States, were aware of the shortcomings of ISI and so had their own reasons for advocating alternative policies.

For a mix of motives, then, Latin America embarked on a new economic approach that had three pillars: macroeconomic stabilization; liberalization, privatization, and a greater role for the private sector; and opening up to foreign trade and capital flows. The best-known version of the model was described in John Williamson's (1990) book on the Washington Consensus. The ten points of the Consensus included stabilization (fiscal discipline, expenditure shift from subsidies to social services, tax broadening, market-based interest rates, and competitive exchange rates); liberalization (privatization, deregulation, and secure property rights); and international opening (trade liberalization and access for FDI). As always, there were differences in the extent to which the new model was adopted. Chile was the first advocate, following the military coup in 1973. Some governments were very aggressive, including Chile, Peru, Bolivia, and Argentina under Menem. Others were somewhat more reluctant: Brazil, Colombia, Costa Rica, Jamaica, and Mexico (Stallings and Peres, 2000).

Stabilization was an important component of the new economic model because many countries had run up large fiscal and balance-of-payments deficits during the 1970s, and inflation was on the rise. These deficits were manageable as long as loans continued, but with the cutoff of lending in 1982, stabilization measures became necessary. Stabilization programs were traditionally designed by the IMF and featured expenditure cuts and perhaps tax increases to reduce fiscal deficits together with devaluations to increase exports, reduce imports, and thus reduce balance-of-payments deficits. If interest rates were raised to combat capital outflows (or attract capital inflows), they would also restrain growth since credit would become more expensive.

More controversial than the macroeconomic stabilization measures, which are typical of economic policy when deficits get out of control, were policies related to the microeconomic management of the domestic economy – privatization and deregulation. Privatization was relevant since many countries had substantially increased the role of state-owned enterprises (SOEs) during the 1970s. Operating behind a wall of protection, the SOEs were generally inefficient and ran large deficits, often financed by international bank loans. Deregulation was meant to unwind much of the red tape put in place over the years, whereby governments "guided" private-sector operations in the productive sphere and with respect to finance.

The third set of measures aimed at opening up the region's economies. The essence of the ISI regime had been the protection of domestic firms from foreign competition. While the protection was initially intended to be temporary, most of it lasted over time as powerful interest groups fought to maintain their privileges. This protection was largely removed as part of the new model, and – equally important – more emphasis was put on exports. At the same time that imports had been restricted under ISI, foreign capital had been invited into the region, often working in conjunction with local private capital and the state. This combination was the heart of dependent development. The nationalizations and expropriations that had taken place in the 1970s, however, had harmed relations with foreign investors. The privatizations brought foreign capital back to the region, and new legislation provided conditions that were attractive to foreign investors. Renegotiations with the banks were aimed at reopening another avenue of finance.

A novel element that accompanied the new economic model was bilateral and plurilateral FTAs. Some were signed with neighbors, but the more important FTAs were with the United States. In 1990, President George H. W. Bush proposed an agreement that would encompass the entire Western Hemisphere (except Cuba). While President Bill Clinton also pushed the proposal without success, he did sign the North American Free Trade Agreement (NAFTA) with Mexico and Canada in 1994; it was followed by an agreement with Chile in 2004 and other countries later. The US FTAs were a way of reinforcing the policies of the new model itself. Indeed, the Mexican president, Carlos Salinas de Gortari, was quite explicit about this aim.

3.3 Dependency and its Impact

I end this section by analyzing the relevance of dependency for understanding Latin America in the second half of the twentieth century. The focus is on the mechanisms of markets, leverage, and linkage to specify how external relations could impact domestic processes and the way in which they interacted with internal actors in the region. Table 1 shows my argument on the relative importance of the three mechanisms of dependency. I argue that dependency generally became more significant in the years after the debt crisis hit Latin America in 1982, although the characteristics changed somewhat.

International markets remained important for Latin American economies after World War II, as they had in the previous century, but the main market for goods shifted from Britain to the United States. For most of the early postwar period, up until the oil shocks of 1973, international markets were quite buoyant. Indeed, some argued that Latin America missed a major opportunity by opting for a closed economy in that period (Gereffi and Wyman, 1990). Since the bond markets remained closed to Latin America because of earlier defaults,

Table 1 Dependency involving the United States and Latin America,
1950–2000

	ISI (1950–80)	New model (1980–2000)
Markets	Medium	High
Leverage	Medium (Political)	High (Economic)
Linkage	Low	Medium

the main source of finance was MNCs. The combination meant that Latin America was dependent on the vagaries of international markets for its growth.

Political leverage was used to combat the wave of nationalism that brought to power a number of governments that wanted to penalize wealthy groups in their own societies and to take control of foreign properties. The response by the US government in several cases was to bring to bear covert (CIA) – or occasionally overt (military) – power to undermine these governments. A new source of potential economic leverage in the postwar period was the IFIs. They provided foreign exchange, but it generally came with strict conditions. The most controversial actor was the IMF, which was tasked with policing macroeconomic policy and particularly balance-of-payments issues.[24] Many governments saw IMF conditionality as encroaching on their policy space, but, for IMF programs to work, it was necessary that they operated in tandem with other creditors. In the 1970s, creditor unity disintegrated when the private banks provided unlimited amounts of unconditional finance. Thus, economic leverage became less important in this period.

External leverage worked best when combined with the participation of local groups, so linkage with business groups, technocrats, and the military were consequential. Linkage between local businesses and MNCs was the basis of the dependent development that Cardoso, Evans, and others described. Both groups shared the goal of rapid growth and high profits from Latin American investments and wanted local governments to help. Political linkage was also important. For example, in the cases of US military or CIA intervention, linkage with local military officials – who had often been trained by their US counterparts – became crucial. And, when governments were overthrown or changed by electoral means, technocrats trained in the United States often assumed key roles in the new, more conservative governments.

With the onset of the debt crisis in 1982, markets assumed a more dominant role that lasted through the next two decades. Most important were financial

---

[24] The IMF began "stand-by programs" in Latin America in the late 1950s; Argentina, Brazil, and Chile alone had engaged in twenty-five programs by the end of the 1960s (Marshall et al., 1983: table 13.1).

markets. While financial markets had provided an enormous volume of loans in the 1970s, those markets were virtually closed to Latin America during the 1980s. The exception was some new loans provided as part of rescheduling agreements negotiated by the IMF. These trends provided the context in which economic leverage could be brought to bear. In the 1990s, foreign capital began to return to the region, but the structural changes that had begun in the 1980s generally continued in conjunction with revived capital flows.

Leverage could be exerted via markets during the debt crisis because of creditor unity, the opposite of the situation in the 1970s. This leverage was jointly asserted by private banks, creditor governments, and IFIs and affected three issue areas in particular. First, debt service was maintained in most cases, especially early in the decade, even when this meant cutting investment and social expenditure. Second, stabilization measures were agreed to and generally implemented. Third, and most important, the ISI model was substituted by a new market-oriented strategy that put the private sector in the dominant position (Stallings, 1992). A new source of leverage in the 1990s, the FTAs that several Latin American countries signed with the United States, embodied conditions with respect to trade in goods and services, intellectual property, and foreign investment (Solis et al., 2009).

Linkage combined to reinforce leverage in this period. The technocrats that assumed government positions following the debt crisis already believed in the need to maintain debt service and undertake macroeconomic stabilization policies. Many of them were advocates of market-oriented policies as well, and the new circumstances presented the opportunity to carry out these policy reforms with less opposition than in the past. The new economic model, of course, provided renewed opportunities for foreign investors and their local allies to work together. A new area of cooperation was in the export sector, which had moved to the center of the economic development strategy of many governments; MNCs could provide access to international markets as well as capital and technology.

How did dependency affect development in the decades after World War II? As a reminder, the Cardoso definition of development that I am using involved the expansion of productive capacity through capital accumulation, technical progress, and the emergence of a working class. Although not specifically included in the definition, it was clear in the Cardoso book – and in the work of others writing from a dependency perspective – that development involved (or even meant) industrialization. This was also the view of ECLA, whose voice was important in the early postwar years, although less so later.

Certainly, the weight of industry in Latin American economies increased from the early 1950s to the end of the 1970s. In addition, the economies became more advanced as they moved into secondary ISI, such that intermediate and capital goods were produced in some countries. The emergence of a sophisticated industrial sector was concentrated in Brazil, Argentina, Mexico, and perhaps Colombia. Chile fostered industry too until the military coup in 1973; afterwards, the government's policies demolished much of the country's industrial capacity in favor of a strategy that relied more heavily on comparative advantage.

With respect to industrialization before the debt crisis in the five countries mentioned, and to a lesser extent in others as well, three arguments can be made. First, with the partial exception of Brazil and Mexico, industries were inefficient because they did not have to face international competition at home or abroad. Second, this inefficiency and low competitiveness were reflected in the lack of industrial exports from the region – again with the partial exception of Brazil and Mexico. This situation contrasted with the experience of East Asian countries, which had experimented with ISI for a short period before adopting export-oriented industrialization strategies (Gereffi and Wyman, 1990). Sluggish exports in Latin America led to continuing balance-of-payments problems and greatly exacerbated the impact of the debt crisis.[25] Third, although dependent development was never expected to benefit the majority of the population, it is important to note that the ISI process was accompanied by very high and in some cases growing inequality (Bulmer-Thomas, 2014: 330–45).

The experience of the region's economies after the debt crisis, and the move from ISI to the new economic model, differed in important ways from the earlier postwar period. In comparison to the lost decade, growth returned, but in a volatile way. Mexico's "tequila crisis" wracked the region in 1995, followed by a 1998–9 banking crisis in Brazil, and Argentina's peso crisis in 2001–2. In addition, the East Asian financial crisis of 1997–8 impacted Latin America at least as much as East Asia itself, where recovery was quite rapid. Table 2 shows a variety of development indicators for Latin America between 1961 and 2003.

Aggregate GDP growth was high under ISI in the 1960s and 1970s, crashed during the 1980s because of the debt crisis, and recovered somewhat under the new model in the 1990s. Investment trends largely mirrored growth trends. Unemployment and poverty also got worse during the debt crisis period, although their trends diverged in the 1990s as poverty fell but unemployment rose (partly because of privatizations during the decade). All trends deteriorated

---

[25] The difference can be seen by the fact that South Korea's debt was about the same magnitude as that of the leading Latin American debtors when measured as a share of GDP. When measured as a share of exports, however, Korea's debt was much smaller, so that Korea did not really suffer a debt crisis in the 1980s.

Table 2 Development trends in Latin America, 1961–2003 (percent)

Years	GDP growth	Investment[a]	Exports[a]	Unemployment[b]	Poverty[c]
1961–70	5.6	20.5	10.3	6.3	NA
1971–80	6.0	23.7	12.4	7.5	40.5
1981–90	1.5	20.6	15.8	8.1	48.4
1991–2000	3.1	20.3	16.6	9.5	43.9
2001–3	0.9	18.6	20.9	11.3	43.5

Sources: World Bank, *World Development Indicators* for GDP, investment, and exports; ECLAC estimates for poverty and unemployment (unpublished).
[a] share of GDP; [b] share of active population; [c] share of total population (dates: 1980, 1990, and average for available years between 1991 and 2002); NA is not available.

after the turn of the century. The composition of growth under the new model was different, with more emphasis on exports, which relied heavily on a new level of partnership with MNCs.

Finally, from the viewpoint of inequality, evidence from a study by the Inter-American Development Bank (1999: 17) indicated that the Gini coefficient fell during the 1970s from around 0.58 to below 0.54 in 1982. During the debt crisis period, by contrast, the Gini rose steadily, and in 1990 exceeded the level of 1970. In the following years, it leveled off. Another study, by the Brookings Institution and UNDP (López-Calva and Lustig, 2010: 6), had a similar message. It said: "Income inequality increased in most Latin American countries during the so-called 'lost decade' of the 1980s and the structural reforms of the early 1990s. Although data availability constrains comprehensive comparison, the evidence suggests that the effects of the debt crisis … were unequalizing." The main reason was that the poor were less able to protect themselves from the austerity policies, and the new economic model distributed benefits in a highly unequal manner.

4 Dependency with Chinese Characteristics?

One of the fundamental assumptions behind dependency theory, made more explicit in the world systems variant, is that the system continues but actors change positions. Especially important is change in hegemon, since that affects the way the system operates due to the structural characteristics of the hegemonic economy and political system and the rules it enforces on others.

Clearly such differences were present when the United States displaced Britain as the hegemonic power after World War II. While both were capitalist democracies, Britain was an island nation with few natural resources and thus reliant on its industries. The need for markets for its goods had been one of the reasons for the formation of the British Empire. The United States, by contrast, was a continental-sized country, rich in natural resources but still developing its industrial sector. Most of its expansion before World War II had consisted of movements to populate the western part of the country. Because of its island status, Britain's security was based on its naval power, while the United States had had a more varied military structure. In the past, the US tendency had been to rely on its geographical location for protection from external threats, but by the end of World War II it had a powerful military apparatus.

China, as an incipient hegemon, shares some characteristics with the United States and Britain, but also differs in significant ways. A continental power with an enormous population, it had a state-dominated economy for millennia, well before Mao Zedong declared the country socialist. The state-dominated economy, in turn, was paired with an authoritarian form of government. China had long been a regional hegemon, with its position enforced by both leverage and linkage. It remains a relatively poor country, which is reliant on others for markets for its increasingly sophisticated industrial goods and for natural resources to keep its factories running and to feed its people. Nonetheless, the aggregate size of its economy and its very impressive growth rates – facilitated by its authoritarian government – have converted China into a potential world hegemonic power.

Scholars have different views on how the increased importance of China might affect the world system. Two such views can be found in the writings of David Harvey (2005) and Giovanni Arrighi (2007). Harvey sees China as simply another neoliberal country ("with Chinese characteristics"), so he does not expect a Chinese hegemon to change things substantially. Arrighi, by contrast, sees China leading a different kind of world order based on South–South cooperation, the declining influence of Northern-dominated institutions and norms, a less ecologically destructive future, and a "commonwealth of civilizations truly respectful of cultural differences" (p. 389). My own view coincides with that of a reviewer of the Arrighi book (Sheppard, 2010). He points out that Arrighi fails to consider a situation in which China could "both challenge the long history of European hegemony and exploit African and Latin American (and Chinese) ecological and human resources." In addition, directly political consequences may accompany a greater role for China. While British and US hegemony were associated with liberal democracy, at least in principle, Chinese leaders believe that their own authoritarian political system is superior.

This section of the Element is a transition from the analysis of the United States and Latin America to the analysis of China and Latin America. The first part takes a broad look at the nature of US hegemony since World War II, focusing on its global scope in both political and economic terms, although the period encompasses less than a century. The second part is a parallel study of China as a regional hegemon for several thousand years; only recently did its vision begin to expand in geographical terms beyond its own region. The third part focuses on China's relations with Southeast Asia and sub-Saharan Africa as the developing areas with which China has had the longest history. The final part asks if China fits a dependency framework with respect to Southeast Asia and sub-Saharan Africa. The last two parts provide a useful background and contrast with China's links with Latin America.

4.1 The United States as Global Hegemon

US hegemony is a recent phenomenon, dating only from the end of World War II. Indeed, the United States as a nation is a recent phenomenon compared to Europe and especially to China. It was not even a regional hegemon until the twentieth century, since Spain and Portugal ruled Latin America as colonial powers for three centuries, and Britain established an informal empire in the region after independence from Iberian control. The declaration of the Monroe Doctrine in 1823 presaged US interest in Latin America, but it had few practical consequences at the time.[26]

Despite the fact that the so-called Spanish–American War gave the United States significant control over the Philippines, Puerto Rico, and Cuba, the country never became a formal colonial power. For much of the period until World War II, the dominant view of US elites was that it was best to stay out of foreign entanglements. This idea went back to colonial times and was embodied in George Washington's farewell address in 1796. Nonetheless, isolationism was a controversial topic that deeply divided US politicians and businesspeople. While many preferred to follow Washington's advice, from the end of the Civil War both economic and political dynamics began to attract the United States into adventures in Europe, Asia, and Latin America. As LaFeber (1989: 181) put it, "As the twentieth century dawned, the US stepped onto the world stage as a great power." Entry into World War I was not popular, however, and only Germany's repeated submarine attacks on US ships brought the country into the conflict. Afterwards the debate resumed. It was epitomized by Wilson's internationalist stance and the Senate's rejection of the Treaty of Versailles together with the refusal to join the League of Nations. Later, the United States had to be dragged into World War II by Franklin Delano Roosevelt.

---

[26] The classic works on Latin America in the colonial and postcolonial periods are the two volumes of the Cambridge Economic History of Latin America (Bulmer-Thomas et al., 2006a, 2006b).

While these divisions made the United States a reluctant hegemon in the interwar years, despite the decline in British power, the stance changed after World War II. The country's overwhelming power vis-à-vis other nations led to a rapid expansion of economic and political relations around the globe. Following the war, the Soviet Union became the United States' main rival, and the ensuing Cold War between the two determined much of US foreign policy. Opposition to communism was crucial to the decision to help Europe (including former enemy Germany) to recover through the Marshall Plan, as was a similar decision to assist Japan and other Asian countries through a large aid program. In the developing world, the United States and the Soviet Union fought over the allegiance of governments to back their respective economic, political, and ideological positions. This process included the US use of military force and covert operations in such well-known cases as the Korean and Vietnamese wars as well as Iran, the Congo, Afghanistan, and a number of Latin American countries, as discussed previously. These military operations were also important to gain access to developing economies for US corporations (Kinzer, 2006).[27]

With the fall of the Soviet Union in 1991, the United States emerged for a few brief years as the "sole superpower," dominant in both economic and military terms. A prominent political scientist (Fukuyama, 1992) argued that this was the end of history, as democracy and capitalism had triumphed over political and economic rivals. Nonetheless, the disappearance of the Soviet Union also undermined US influence, as allies in industrial and developing countries alike began to take more independent positions in the absence of a common enemy. Economic competition and differences of opinion about security policy emerged between the United States and Europe as well as Asia. The rise of China, to which we now turn, was an important part of this narrative.

4.2 China as Regional Hegemon

The story of US expansion after 1945, as summarized in the previous paragraphs and Section 3 of the Element, is well known among Latin Americanists and other students of Western history. Less well known are details of the Chinese experience leading up to its challenge to the US role in the world in the twenty-first century. While there is little space here to analyze the Chinese trajectory, a few points must be made to highlight the contrast between China

---

[27] Kinzer (2006: 3) remarks on the "quirk of history" that the United States became a great power at the same time that MNCs (often based in the United States) were becoming important players in world affairs.

and the United States and to lay the basis for analyzing China's relations with Latin America.

China was the dominant power in Asia and, arguably, the most advanced area of the world for several thousand years. Imperial China was a cultural center of the first order. Great construction works were also notable, and China was responsible for many scientific contributions that Europe only began to match much later.[28] Not surprisingly, over this very lengthy period, China began to see itself as the most important part of the world: the central (or middle) kingdom. It presided over a tribute area that encompassed much of modern-day East, Central, and South Asia.[29]

In the nineteenth century, however, China's dominion began to unravel. Angus Maddison (2007) estimated that China was the largest economy in the world in 1820. Ravaged militarily and socially by the opium wars (1839–42, 1856–60), China's share of global GDP had fallen by half as of 1870. With internal rebellion and external incursions, it was only a matter of time until the Qing dynasty fell in 1912. In 1931, Japan invaded Manchuria and occupied much of the country thereafter. Only in 1945, after Japan's defeat in World War II, did the occupation of China end. The Chinese often refer to the period between 1839 and 1949 as the "century of humiliation." It is this dual heritage that is the essential background for China's current struggle to regain its preeminence in Asia and to increase its role in the broader international system.

From a modern perspective, the major turning point in Chinese history was the end of the civil war between communists and nationalists and the declaration of the People's Republic in 1949. Mao Zedong, as chairman of the Chinese Communist Party (CCP), became the supreme ruler of the country until his death in 1976. This period saw the new China, under a command economy, emerge through traumatic ups and downs, including the Great Leap Forward and the Cultural Revolution. A second turning point came in December 1978, when the Central Committee of the Communist Party designated Deng Xiaoping as the paramount leader.[30] Deng set China on a new path that combined Communist Party rule with economic reforms and opening, creating a socialist market economy ("socialism with Chinese characteristics"). The result was a dramatic increase in economic growth and a significant decrease

---

[28] Joseph Needham, the preeminent historian of China's role in science, wrote a multivolume history of China's contributions. Needham (1954) is the introduction to the series.

[29] Of course, the literature on imperial China is vast and cannot be summarized here. As an introduction, by a journalist who has written extensively on China, see French (2017).

[30] Deng was never president of China or general secretary of the CCP. Of the top three titles, the only one he held was head of the Central Military Commission; his power was informal.

in poverty. At the same time, an important aspect of Deng's leadership style was his call for China to be modest about its achievements.

The third turning point was the rise of Xi Jinping. When Xi became general secretary of the CCP in 2012 and president of China in 2013, it was expected that he would follow Deng in accelerating economic reforms, expanding the use of markets, and increasing international opening. The most optimistic hoped he might take steps toward political liberalization. Soon, however, indications of economic backsliding began to appear. In addition, Xi demanded more control for the Communist Party, stifling press freedoms that had emerged under his predecessors as well as academic freedom in universities. Xi became sufficiently dominant in China's political system that the People's National Congress in 2018 voted to remove term limits on the presidency, meaning that he could serve as president for life.

To understand the implications for China's relations with developing countries, it is important to examine the economic trends deriving from these policy changes. China was not always a rich or a high-growth country. Indeed, in 1949, it was extremely poor; per capita GNP was estimated at US$50 in 1952. From 1961 to 1968, the average growth rate was a mere 1.7 percent, as the economy was held back by political turmoil. From 1969 to 1982, shortly after the change in economic paradigm, average growth reached 8.2 percent. Only in the nearly four-decade period from 1982 to 2010 did China's reputation for spectacular growth emerge – the economy grew 10.3 percent per year, before slowing to 7.5 percent from 2011 to 2016.

As a result of these trends, by 2016, China had become the second largest economy in the world (the largest in purchasing power parity [PPP] terms) as well as the largest exporter. Nonetheless, its per capita GDP (around US$8,000) put it in the upper-middle income category. China's export basket was shifting toward more high-tech goods, while its imports were divided between raw materials (mainly from developing countries) and inputs for its exports (as part of its role as an assembly hub in the Asian division of labor). It was both among the largest recipients of FDI and, more recently, the largest foreign investors. In the social area, there remained a vast gap between urban and rural areas, despite the achievement of lifting some 800 million people out of poverty, according to World Bank estimates. Major and persistent problems included high inequality, pollution, and social unrest.[31]

In the economic sphere, two domestic initiatives were particularly important under Xi. First was emphasis on moving the economy toward a "new normal." The new normal would involve lower growth rates, accompanied by structural shifts from reliance on investment and exports toward more emphasis on

---

[31] The main English-language source on the Chinese economy is Naughton (2006, 2018).

consumption, and from an economy that emphasized manufacturing toward a greater role for services. Such changes have major implications for China's trade partners from developed and developing countries alike. Second, President Xi set out an agenda called "Made in China 2025," which aimed to make China a world leader in innovation in ten high-tech sectors of the economy and to make it less dependent on foreign technology. This transformation would be aided by coordination across the government, the private sector, and academia; large subsidies for favored firms; and training of required labor.[32]

The new development model adopted after Deng assumed power in 1978 also led to changes in China's international relations, which had been geared toward the Soviet Union until the 1960s and followed by a period of closure to the world. The main exceptions were China's replacement of Taiwan in the UN in 1971 and the opening to the United States the following year. Deng's policies brought a gradual liberalization of imports and a focus on labor-intensive exports to pay for these imports. Export processing and FDI became the motor of Chinese growth. Other sources of finance were also sought. Diplomatic normalization between Japan and China took place in 1972; after 1978, China became one of the largest recipients of Japan's aid program, and Japan became China's largest bilateral donor. Multilateral agencies, especially the World Bank, were also significant donors (Stallings and Kim, 2017: chp. 4).

By the mid-1990s, China's economy was booming, and the Chinese government was becoming more confident in its international approach. While China was accumulating large amounts of reserves through its trade surpluses, and attracting large amounts of incoming FDI, it had virtually no investment of its own abroad.[33] In 1999, the "Go Out Policy" (or the Going Global Strategy) was announced, which encouraged large Chinese firms to undertake investment projects abroad. Initial investments were in the Asian region and in Africa; natural resources were the main sector of interest because of China's need for raw materials.

Another initiative of this period was the resumption of China's foreign aid program. Despite China's poverty in the 1950s, it ran a generous foreign aid program to help fellow socialist countries. Three principles were established that continue to guide China's aid today: equality between donor and recipient, mutual benefit, and "no strings attached." While the program never completely closed down, it was much less active during the 1980s and early 1990s. The new approach was substantially different than the earlier foreign aid. No longer were decisions made on the basis of politics and ideology, but on a business basis with

---

[32] The United States and some other countries argue that the program will also involve pilfering intellectual property.

[33] An exception was China's first investment in Peru's mining sector (Guo, 2015).

an eye to supporting the Chinese economy. In addition to its neighbors, the other main recipients in this period were in Africa, where China became the main donor by the early 2000s (Bräutigam, 2011).

Accession to the World Trade Organization (WTO) in 2001 was the most important international undertaking of these years. China had to accept a broad range of regulatory changes to harmonize with international standards, and accession required promises of major opening to foreign companies in many sectors. Nonetheless, China's leadership thought WTO membership was crucial since it would lock in the reforms enacted since 1978 and give China greatly expanded access to international markets (Lardy, 2002). And, as it turned out, many of the promises were not kept, so China got the advantages of membership without paying all of the costs.

With Xi Jinping's arrival on the scene, further foreign policy changes took place. His vision of a "rejuvenated" China, regaining its rightful place in the world, was the framework for the specific programs he initiated. In the process, Xi abandoned Deng's admonition to be modest about the country's aims and said that he planned to "make China's voice heard, and inject more Chinese elements into international rules" (Economy, 2018: 190).

His most important international project is the vast Belt and Road Initiative (BRI), announced in 2013. Basically an infrastructure program, the plan is to construct overland and maritime transport links to connect more than one hundred countries. The amounts of money involved are unclear; although some talk of a trillion dollars or more, Chinese officials have spoken of US $250 billion (Economy, 2018: 191). While many countries, especially in the developing world, have been eager to gain access to the large-scale funds involved in the BRI, anxiety and skepticism have also arisen. On the one hand, governments worry that, since the projects are so large, they will give China too much power over recipient countries and their policies. On the other hand, the size of the projects and the loans to finance them can lead to debt crises in recipient countries.[34] This has already happened in Sri Lanka, where China took over a port and land around it when the government could not meet loan payments (Abi-Habib, 2018). Several Asian governments – including Malaysia, Myanmar, and Pakistan – have renegotiated or canceled projects with China because of worries about high debt implications.[35]

---

[34] The anxiety about debt issues is reinforced by the lack of transparency. A new study (Horn et al., 2019) says that about half of China's lending is not reported to international agencies that collect such information. Because of these concerns as well as issues of corruption, Xi promised at the second meeting of BRI countries in Beijing in April 2019 to revamp BRI procedures. See Zhang (2019).

[35] A parallel initiative, which has tried to avoid the transparency problems of the BRI, is the Asian Infrastructure Investment Bank (AIIB). While initially conceived as a Chinese bank, complaints

4.3 China's Relations with Southeast Asia and Sub-Saharan Africa

To highlight some of the impacts of China's reemergence onto the global stage and to provide a useful comparison for the study of China and Latin America, I conclude this section with a very brief look at China's relations with Southeast Asia and sub-Saharan Africa. These are the developing regions with which China has the longest and deepest history, so my theme of "dependency with Chinese characteristics" can best be introduced in this context. The nature of China's relationships with various countries in the two regions differs due to geopolitics, as China is obviously more dominant in the case of Asian countries. Also, of course, countries in both regions are heterogeneous with respect to resource endowment, level of development, and political system. Nonetheless, there are important similarities in China's economic relations with Asia and Africa.[36]

China is now the main trade partner with most countries in both regions. In most cases in Africa and many in Southeast Asia, these countries export raw materials to China in exchange for industrial goods, which is the old colonial pattern replicated in the twenty-first century. A result is that local industries in these countries have not been able to compete. In the more advanced Southeast Asian countries, local firms have been incorporated into regional supply chains led by Chinese companies – although generally at the low end of the chains – as part of the new Asian division of labor. Initially, inputs were shipped to China for assembly, but, with wages rising in China, some Southeast Asian countries have become assembly hubs.

Closely related to trade patterns is China's FDI in these regions. After the Go Out Policy began, trade, FDI, and loans became linked. The mechanism for countries with strong natural resource endowments was simple: Chinese firms, almost always SOEs, made investments in Southeast Asia and Africa – especially in petroleum, but also metals and agricultural crops. Frequently, they imported Chinese workers, rather than employing locals, which increased local employment problems. In general, the outputs of these projects were exported

---

led to ownership open to any country that wanted to join. Most major industrial countries and some developing countries have done so, with the prominent exceptions of the United States and Japan. To provide legitimacy for AIIB, the bank's leadership has hired personnel from the World Bank and regional banks, set out public criteria for loans that are similar to those of the other IFIs, and cofinanced its first projects with them. Seven Latin American countries have indicated an interest in joining.

[36] This section draws on many (English-language) sources. There is an extensive literature on China and Africa. See, for example, Brautigam (2011), Shinn and Eisenman (2012), Taylor (2014), and Alden and Large (2019). The best data source on China and Africa is the China–Africa Research Initiative of Johns Hopkins University (www.sais-cari.org). Information on China and Southeast Asia is more scattered. On political and economic relations, see Goh (2016), Denoon (2017), Heginbotham (2018), Stallings (2018), and Stromseth (2019). On security issues, see Swaine and Fravel (2011).

back to China, which gave the host countries access to foreign exchange. At the same time, the bundling of trade and investment led to complaints about pricing and generally about the lack of transparency and accusations of corruption.

In addition to investments in natural resources, Chinese SOEs also have also invested in infrastructure projects – roads, railroads, bridges, ports, airports – which are needed to get the products back to China or occasionally to third markets. Electricity is another kind of infrastructure that is often lacking in the two regions, so building dams and hydroelectric plants are common activities undertaken by Chinese firms. Both transport and electricity could be valuable for local use as well as for trade, although there have been complaints that access or prices made this difficult. Another type of investment has involved real estate, whereby Chinese firms get licenses to buy land to construct (usually expensive) housing. People who had been living on the land are frequently thrown off with little or no compensation, while the housing is geared for upper middle-class residents – often Chinese buyers.[37]

A third type of economic relationship involves loans from Chinese institutions to local entities, usually governments. These might be foreign aid – sometimes grants or zero-interest loans, but increasingly concessional loans with lower than market interest rates and/or longer maturities – or they might involve commercial loans at market prices. The loans often go to finance projects undertaken by Chinese SOEs, so the money is merely transferred from one bank account to another in China rather than going to the host government that is formally the borrower and responsible for repayment. One of the most-discussed effects of these loans is the accumulation of large amounts of debt, which can overwhelm smaller economies. Even a regional powerhouse like Malaysia has become concerned with potential debt issues and, after a recent change in political leadership, canceled or postponed several Chinese projects.

One of the original principles of Chinese foreign aid, and Chinese funding more broadly, is that it comes without conditions. Of course there are conditions – the country must recognize the PRC rather than its rival, Taiwan, and the product must be available for sale to China. But the types of conditions that are often put on Western loans, such as economic policy or political requirements, are not applied. While the lack of conditionality, and the policy of noninterference in domestic issues of other countries, are attractive to developing countries, this has also tarnished China's international reputation since the PRC offers aid to some of the worst human rights violators in both regions. Environmental and labor conditionality are rarely applied, which has caused

---

[37] See Elten (2018) for a discussion of Chinese electricity and real estate investment in Cambodia.

protests from workers and other citizens demanding greater protection. Another demand is for greater transparency with respect to the terms of Chinese projects. The strong suspicion is that corruption – involving both local and Chinese participants – is significant.

While economic characteristics are similar in Asia and Africa, political and even military activities complicate relations between China and some of its Asian neighbors. China's demands for control over certain territories or water bodies have led to conflicts with neighbors. Five nations in addition to China lay claim to all or part of the Spratly and the Parcel Islands in the South China Sea. These claims are important for economic reasons, including oil and fishing, as well as control of shipping lanes that pass through the area. China has been heavy-handed in trying to enforce its claims, but Southeast Asian countries are reluctant to challenge their main economic partner. Until recently, China had not had military bases outside the country, but a first one was constructed in 2016 in Djibouti (on the Horn of Africa) and another has been rumored in Cambodia (Reed, 2019). Although Chinese officials say the Djibouti base is for logistical purposes for participation in peacekeeping operations, and does not violate their noninterference policy, it has set a precedent. The large-scale Chinese investment in ports in Southeast Asia and sub-Saharan Africa has also caused concern. While the stated purpose is commercial, military use is possible in the future (Shepard, 2017).

4.4 Dependency with Chinese Characteristics

Two questions are of interest with respect to these relationships. Do they constitute relations of dependency, as defined earlier in the Element? And do they promote or hinder development in the two regions? With respect to dependency, Table 3 shows the three elements of the dependency framework presented earlier; it can be compared to Table 1 on US–Latin American relations.

China turned to the use of markets in a significant way with Deng's reform and opening policies. It trades in international markets, and it offers and receives finance through international markets. Nonetheless, the lack of transparency in many of its transactions with other countries, especially developing countries, can distort the operation of markets in international relations and provide the opportunity to exert economic leverage. In addition, markets within China for labor and credit are geared to favor SOEs, which has implications for China's international transactions.

Leverage is the central mechanism used by China to create dependency relationships in Asia and Africa. China makes use of the enormous difference

Table 3 Dependency involving China with Southeast Asia and sub-Saharan Africa, 1980–2018

	Southeast Asia	**Sub-Saharan Africa**
Markets	Low	Low
Leverage	High (Political)	Medium (Political)
Linkage	Low	Low

in the size of its economy and its political power to enforce its economic requirements on developing countries. This has meant that developing countries produce and sell raw materials to China, regardless of the problems this kind of activity is known to create. On the other side of the trade relationship, SOE sales of industrial goods make it extremely difficult for local firms to compete, especially when dumping is involved. The use of Chinese labor to carry out projects prevents significant employment generation. Pressure is also brought to bear for political compliance, whether in terms of the One-China Policy or backing China in international and regional organizations. In Asia, military force has been used in the past against South Korea and Vietnam; more recently, economic boycotts and military pressures have been used if economic incentives are insufficient.

Linkage is projected through the idea of China's "peaceful rise" and its narrative of South–South cooperation. In Africa, presidential visits and the triennial Forum for China–Africa Cooperation (FOCAC) are important symbols of friendship and respect. Likewise, the use of exchanges of various kinds is significant, especially educational exchanges where African students predominate in such programs at Chinese universities. From time to time, China has also undertaken "charm offensives" in Southeast Asia (Kurlantzick, 2008), but these periods tend not to last long (Leaf, 2014; Pei, 2018). Examples include the preferences given to ASEAN countries in the context of their FTA negotiations or the loans promised to the region. While China has an interest in good relations with its Southeast Asian neighbors, leverage is often substituted for linkage.

There is a strong, ongoing debate about development in the relationship between China and these countries. Proponents of the Chinese presence insist that economic relations with China have led to increased growth in Africa and Asia and thus improvement in the lives of their citizens. It is true that growth has been high, especially for raw materials providers during the China Boom, but the quality of growth is of concern. Critics focus on the negative aspects of the relationship – volatility, inequality, corruption, and the enormous power differential that takes initiative away from local governments – but they do not have an alternative strategy. The fact that Western presence in the two regions generally did not lead to positive outcomes in the past partially offsets criticisms of China's role.

I would argue that a dependency framework is useful for analyzing China's relationships with its nearest neighbors. It provides insights into the nature of the highly asymmetrical links China maintains with Southeast Asia and sub-Saharan Africa and the problematic impact on the economies of the region. If we look back to the discussion by Cardoso and Faletto, it will be remembered that their main concern is that dependency hinders self-sustaining growth in developing countries. This appears to be true in these two regions.

Of course, it would be misleading to assume that all of the problems of the two regions are due to China. Such as approach is antithetical to the Cardoso–Faletto version of dependency. Any analysis of development in the two regions must put heavy emphasis on the characteristics of the respective governments and other domestic actors; the poor level of governance and high amounts of corruption in the societies themselves are a major part of their problems. To get a better understanding of the relationship between external and internal factors in Southeast Asia and sub-Saharan Africa, as well as the variation within the two regions, would require detailed investigation of individual cases. Nonetheless, these brief sketches can provide useful background – and perhaps contrast – to China's relations with Latin America, to which we now turn.

5 China–Latin America Economic Relations

The virtual explosion of Latin America's economic relations with China constitutes one of the most dramatic changes in the region's history. A useful starting point is the year 2000. At that time, trade and financial links between the two sides were minimal. Less than two decades later, China has become the main trading partner of several South American countries and the second largest of several others. It is also one of the largest sources of FDI and loans for the region. Moreover, Latin America is a frequent destination for top Chinese leaders, and new Latin American presidents hasten to schedule visits to Beijing. Thousands of Latin American students are studying Mandarin in Confucius Institutes in Latin America itself or taking classes in Chinese universities or other training programs.

Given the magnitude and speed of these changes, many questions are being asked by scholars, policymakers, and the general public. Why and how did the new relationship develop? What are its main elements? Will the relationship last? What are the costs and benefits? Who is winning? Who is losing? Are there ways to maximize the benefits while minimizing the costs? In this section, I examine data related to some of these questions to provide an interpretive framework for the new relationship. In particular, I ask if dependency offers a useful approach to understanding the changes that have come about.

The answer I provide in the remainder of the Element is that a dependency framework is useful in two ways. On the one hand, it helps to reveal how external and internal forces interacted to produce economic and social outcomes in the context of a growing Chinese role in Latin America. On the other hand, it shows how these forces – discussed in terms of markets, leverage, and linkage – differed from the classical dependency formulation of US–Latin American relations and also from China's relations with Southeast Asia and sub-Saharan Africa. Latin American countries themselves are divided into two groups: those with transparent policies operating under the rule of law and those where policy decisions are typically made in backrooms without legal procedures to guide them. In the latter case, leverage is more important than markets in determining outcomes and vice versa. That leverage, however, operated through economic rather than political channels, as was often the case with the United States. Another distinction in timing is also relevant. Early in the twenty-first century, the booming Chinese economy stimulated high growth in Latin America, so that markets alone could produce outcomes of mutual benefit. Once the boom ended, China's government had to step in to prevent negative spillover from damaging the relationship. In the absence of political leverage possibilities, they stepped up the creation and use of linkage to bolster economic ties.

A snapshot of the socioeconomic situation in Latin America at the beginning of the twenty-first century establishes a baseline for the analysis. The timeline picks up where the discussion of US–Latin American relations ended in Section 3. I then turn to an analysis of trade relations during the so-called China Boom (roughly 2003–13) as well as the recession that followed as trade with China fell off. A complementary analysis focuses on financial flows from China to Latin America, including FDI, policy bank loans, and foreign aid. I finish with an analysis of the impact of these new relationships.

5.1 Latin America in the Early Twenty-First Century

Latin America's economy was in the doldrums by the early 2000s. While the experience with the new market-oriented model in the 1990s had produced some successes, events both in the region and beyond had made the trajectory quite volatile. As seen earlier in Table 2, the average GDP growth rate for the decade was a solid 3.1 percent, although this had been undermined by the Mexican and East Asian financial crises. In 2001–3, however, just before the China Boom began, growth averaged only 0.9 percent per year. The region's always low investment rate was falling (20.3 percent of GDP on average in the 1990s versus 18.6 percent in 2001–3). Not surprisingly, unemployment was on the rise in comparison with the 1990s (9.5 percent versus 11.3 percent), although poverty remained roughly the same. Only exports seemed to be providing a bright spot as they continued to rise as a share of GDP in comparison with previous decades (16.6 percent of GDP versus 20.9 percent).

These problematic trends had to be seen in light of the shift in development model from a relatively closed economy to a more open model. Was it just a question of more time needed to adjust to the changes so as to reap the rewards of the new policies? Were lackluster results related to poor implementation? Or were the policies themselves the cause of the problems? Debates about these alternative explanations were strong and sometimes bitter, since the new model remained very controversial. In addition, if the third alternative was correct, there remained the issue of what kind of changes were needed. Few wanted to return to the ISI policies per se, but the idea was prevalent that some adjustments were needed.

Moreover, the economic debate took place within a political context that made it especially compelling. Beginning with the election of Hugo Chávez in Venezuela in 1998, followed by Ricardo Lagos in Chile (2000), Luiz Inácio Lula da Silva in Brazil (2003), and Néstor Kirchner in Argentina (2003), governments with leftist ideologies came to power. Later, they were joined by Evo Morales in Bolivia (2006) and Rafael Correa in Ecuador (2007). While differing in their specific characteristics, all of these leaders were looking for ways to distinguish themselves from their conservative predecessors, to get their countries growing again, and to make progress in dealing with poverty and inequality (Levitsky and Roberts, 2011). It was these governments, under these political and economic circumstances, that welcomed the unexpected new relationship with China.

Before moving to the China relationship per se, it should be noted that well before the China Boom began, some experts and policymakers had been looking to East Asia as a source of lessons on how countries there achieved such rapid growth amidst relatively equal income distribution. In the mid-1980s and 1990s, interest centered on Japan, South Korea, Taiwan, and some Southeast Asian countries. A large literature focused initially on development strategies, noting that both regions had experimented with ISI, but that East Asia had turned more quickly to export-oriented industrialization (Gereffi and Wyman, 1990). Later, studies were conducted on sectors and particular policy areas. Hypotheses to account for East Asia's success included the role of the state, more open economies, and the emphasis on human capital (Birdsall and Jasperson, 1997).

5.2 China–Latin America Trade Relations

Some trade existed between China and selected Latin American countries before the boom started. In 1990, based on Latin American figures,[38] Latin America and the Caribbean exported US$841 million of goods to China and imported US$604 million, leading to a small surplus. Ten years later, that picture had changed in several important ways. First, exports had increased to US$3.7 billion, while imports had burgeoned to US$8.3 billion. Second, Latin America had a sizeable trade deficit with China. Third, China represented 0.6 percent of total Latin American trade in 1990, while, by 2000, the figure had risen to 1.6 percent.[39] Nonetheless, it was clear that China had not yet become a major trade partner.

As a measure of China's dramatically increased relevance for Latin America during the early 2000s, total trade rose from US$12 billion in 2000 to a peak of US$268 billion in 2013 (see Figure 1). This trade, however, was very unequally distributed across the region. Some 43 percent of Latin American exports in 2013 came from Brazil, 18 percent from Chile, 12 percent from Venezuela, and 7 percent from Peru; thus, these four countries alone accounted for 80 percent of the total. Imports were more evenly spread across the region; the top four importers represented 68 percent of the total. The largest importer was Mexico (33 percent), followed by Brazil (20 percent), Chile (9 percent), and Argentina (6 percent), which meant that the large deficit that Latin America had with China in 2013 – over US$80 billion – was largely accounted for by Mexico, although many countries had smaller deficits.[40] Another way of looking at the importance of trade with China was that, by 2013, it had displaced the United States as the largest export market for Argentina, Brazil, Chile, and Peru; it was the second largest market for several other countries.

This pattern of exports and imports was determined by the so-called commodity lottery (Blattman et al., 2007). The large majority of natural resources were located in South America – oil in Venezuela and Ecuador, copper in Chile and Peru, iron ore in Brazil, and soybeans in Brazil and Argentina. These were the products that China needed most: oil and metals to keep its economy running at double-digit growth rates and soybeans to provide animal feed and

---

[38] There are substantial differences in trade data as presented by Latin America and China. Both the IMF and the UN's Comtrade show much larger deficits based on Latin American data. The reasons remain to be determined.

[39] Calculated from IMF, *Direction of Trade Statistics*.

[40] Calculated from IMF, *Direction of Trade Statistics*.

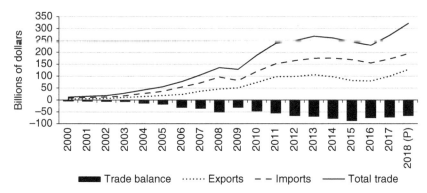

Figure 1 Trade between China and Latin America, 2000–18 (billions of dollars)
Source: ECLAC, Division of International Trade and Integration (unpublished).

thus satisfy the demand for meat by a rising middle class. Small quantities of luxury food items were also sought from Latin America. For the region as a whole (excluding Mexico), five products accounted for 75 percent of exports to China. It is notable that this concentration was not representative of the overall export basket, but unique to trade with China. Together, in 2013, exports of primary products and natural-resource–based manufactures were more than 90 percent for the China market, while less than 60 percent for the world as a whole. Imports from China were mainly high-tech manufactured products (over 40 percent) and medium-tech manufactures (30 percent); from the world, about 55 percent fell into these categories (ECLAC, 2015).

These two factors – a skewed distribution of countries and a high concentration in a few commodities – severely limited the benefits that the region received even in the best of times. A particular concern was Mexico, together with Central America. Few of Mexico's exports were of interest to China since the two countries had a competitive rather than a complementary relationship like South America had. Moreover, China's cost advantage enabled it to displace Mexico from the crucial US market as well as creating problems in the Mexican market itself. But even the South American "winners" were worried about the implications of this boom in trade with China. They had spent decades building up their industries, only to see them unable to compete, and their export baskets begin to look more like those of the nineteenth century than the twentieth. This had implications for many aspects of development, as I will discuss later.

An important aspect of the China–Latin America trade relationship during the boom years was the move to institutionalize these links through FTAs. China's first ever FTA with a single country was with Chile. A particular aim on the Chilean side was to establish a strong legal framework for its trade with

China, given concerns about the rule of law in that country. The agreement was signed in 2005. It covered only goods, unlike the broader agreements that Chile typically signed, but the treaty anticipated future negotiations on services and investment. A dispute mechanism was included together with intellectual property and several social topics. The FTA provided for immediate duty-free entry for the large majority of Chilean exports into China, but Chilean industrialists were concerned about competition with China, so a number of China's industrial exports were put on the ten-year list, as were Chilean fish and fruit (Stallings, 2009). Between 2005 and 2013, trade between the two countries more than quadrupled from US$8 billion to US$35 billion (Wise, 2016: 86).

Peru followed Chile in negotiating an FTA, as it has followed Chile in so many economic policies in the last two decades. Its agreement was signed in 2009. According to Wise (2016: 96), Peru got better terms than its Chilean neighbors had managed to negotiate, including a larger share of immediate duty-free exports and protection for more "sensitive products" in the industrial sector. Separate chapters on investment and services were included in the treaty itself, as was a dispute settlement clause. Trade essentially doubled between the signing of the agreement and the end of the boom period, expanding from US $7.6 billion to US$16.6 billion – but the total was less than half of the Chilean trade in the same year.

Costa Rica's FTA with China, signed in 2010, came about in a different way than the other two. Costa Rica shifted its diplomatic relations from Taiwan to the PRC in 2007 and was rewarded with large quantities of resources, ranging from various public works projects to a US$1 billion joint-venture refinery. In addition, the recognition of China led to a third FTA between China and a Latin American country. China's hope was that the demonstration effect of the resource flow would convince other countries to follow Costa Rica's diplomatic lead (Stallings, 2017). Costa Rica's export basket is also quite different from those of Chile and Peru. Partly as a result of the decision by Intel to locate an important plant in Costa Rica in the late 1990s, the country became a hub for high-tech production. Thus, the opportunity to gain privileged access to the enormous China market for its industrial exports was extremely attractive. Nonetheless, by the end of the boom, not much of an increase had occurred.

Just as trade was the main mechanism that underpinned the China Boom, it was also the main mechanism through which economic relations between China and Latin America suffered when the boom ended. Regional exports to China fell from a high of US$106 billion in 2013 to a low of US$78 billion in 2016 (a decline of more than 25 percent) before beginning to recover the following year. The largest loser in absolute terms was Brazil (24 percent and US$11 billion) between 2013 and 2016, but by far the biggest loser in percentage terms was

Venezuela (71 percent and US$9 billion). Other commodity exporters, such as Chile, Peru, and Argentina, also suffered significant losses. The regional deficit actually increased since exports fell more than imports. Deficits were very unevenly distributed across countries. Only Brazil, Venezuela, Chile, and Peru had surpluses in 2016. The Caribbean nations had small deficits, while Central American countries had somewhat larger ones. Overall, the largest deficits were found in Argentina, Colombia, and especially Mexico.[41]

Little changed between the boom and post-boom years in the composition of trade. About 70 percent of Latin American exports to China continued to be primary products with another 20 percent natural-resource–based manufactures. On the import side, industrial goods continued to dominate. A very high level of concentration in export composition also continued; the top five products alone accounted for nearly 70 percent of the total. An additional fifteen – mainly mining, petroleum, and some forestry and agricultural products – constituted another 15 percent, so the top twenty represented 85 percent of the total, a much higher concentration than exports to the rest of the world. For example, ECLAC (2018: 42) reports that the number of products exported to the Latin American regional market exceeded the number exported to China by more than ten times.

5.3 China–Latin America Financial Relations

While trade is the best known and best documented aspect of China's economic relations with Latin America, the export of capital has been equally important. China's outgoing FDI is a more recent phenomenon than trade, and the data are much less reliable.[42] According to ECLAC, Chinese FDI began to come into the region in significant amounts in 2005, accelerating after the financial crisis in 2008. From 2005 until the China Boom ended in 2013, total FDI inflows from China were nearly US$60 billion or an average of US$6.5 billion per year (see Figure 2). Chinese FDI was around 5 percent of Latin America's FDI from all sources in this period.

---

[41] Calculated from IMF, *Direction of Trade Statistics.*

[42] Unless otherwise indicated, all data discussed in this subsection are unpublished estimates from ECLAC's Unit of Investment and Corporate Strategies, on the basis of Bloomberg and the *Financial Times'* FDI Markets (provided to the author in January 2019, updated August 2019). These estimates differ somewhat from previously published ECLAC data. There are multiple sources of data on Chinese FDI to Latin America, which are relatively consistent over time but vary from year to year depending on underlying data sources and if investments are recorded when announced or completed. In addition to ECLAC, sources include the American Enterprise Institute, the Atlantic Council, and a monitoring service at the National Autonomous University of Mexico (managed by Enrique Dussel Peters). The main Chinese source of outward FDI, published annually by the Ministry of Commerce, has very different figures for Latin America.

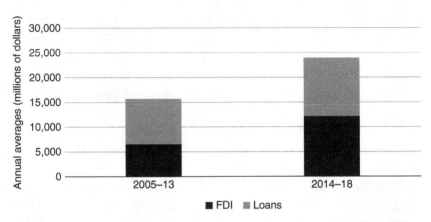

Figure 2 Chinese finance to Latin America, annual averages, 2005–18 (millions of dollars)

Sources: ECLAC, Unit of Investment and Corporate Strategies (for FDI); Inter-American Dialogue, China–Latin America Finance Database (for loans).

Of the total amount, 45 percent represented new projects (greenfield investment), and 55 percent came from the purchase of existing assets (mergers and acquisitions [M&As]). The Chinese are more interested in M&A transactions, since they provide access to successful, ongoing companies. For the host countries, in contrast, greenfield operations are more valuable, since they result in increased production capacity, rather than merely change of ownership. Greenfield projects by Chinese companies were more numerous but substantially smaller in amount than M&A investments. The average size between 2005 and 2013 were US$157 million versus US$617 million, respectively.

As with trade, the distribution of FDI across countries was very uneven. Over half (56 percent) went to Brazil alone, followed by Argentina (11 percent) and Peru (10 percent). Thus, the top three recipients accounted for 77 percent of Chinese FDI inflows to the region in 2005–13. Concentration also occurred by sector and individual project. ECLAC estimates that 63 percent of Chinese investments in the boom period were in natural resources (coal, oil, gas, mining); in comparison, only 25 percent of total foreign investment inflows into the region involved natural resources. In the peak years of 2010–11, 60 percent of Chinese investment went to purchase mining and petroleum assets in Brazil and Argentina; other major oil investments were in Colombia, Ecuador, and Venezuela; all were made by China's four state-owned oil majors. Mining investments were more concentrated, as all were in Brazil or Peru.

Other sectors included utilities, where the biggest investments through 2013 were in electricity in Brazil via a Chinese firm entering the Brazilian market by acquiring assets from Spanish companies. Investments in agriculture were limited. One Chinese firm invested in soybean processing in Brazil, and a few small Chilean vineyards were purchased to export wine to China. In manufacturing, it is of note that the few Chinese firms that showed interest in Latin America followed the same path as US MNCs in the 1960s and 1970s. They wanted to produce for the domestic market in Latin America, and especially Brazil (ECLAC, 2015: 59–65). An important example was autos, where assembly boomed before Brazil's economic downturn.

In addition to FDI, the other main source of capital flows from China to Latin America involved loans from Chinese banks, particularly the two main government-owned "policy banks": China Development Bank (CDB) and China Export-Import Bank (CHEXIM). Data on these flows have been gathered by Kevin Gallagher and colleagues at Boston University and diffused through a website at the Inter-American Dialogue (www.thedialogue.org). The data sources are newspapers and other public announcements; these have been criticized, but the database provides the best information available given the lack of transparency on the Chinese side.

According to these data, Chinese policy bank loans started in 2005 on a very small scale. Between 2005 and 2013, however, substantial amounts of money were transferred with a total of US$82 billion, compared to US$60 billion in FDI. As has frequently been pointed out, the amount was also more than the World Bank and the Inter-American Development Bank (IDB) together loaned to Latin America (Gallagher et al., 2012). While the loans were again very concentrated by country, the mix of recipients was different. Four borrowers represented 92 percent of all loans to the region between 2005 and 2013: Venezuela (60 percent), Argentina (13 percent), Brazil (10 percent), and Ecuador (9 percent). With the partial exception of Brazil, the main loan recipients were countries that could not access international capital markets because of their policies, high risk, and ideological stance. China was happy to step into the breach. For the period 2005–13, 52 percent of loans went to finance oil, gas, coal, mining, and renewable energy projects and 18 percent for infrastructure (mainly transportation). More than 28 percent, however, provided budgetary support and discretionary finance (in Venezuela and Ecuador), suggesting a lack of due diligence on the part of Chinese lenders.[43]

---

[43] I have disaggregated Inter-American Dialogue data, provided to me on a loan-by-loan basis, so my categories are somewhat different than theirs. In particular, they consider that nearly all of the China–Venezuela Joint Fund proceeds went for energy. A closer examination suggests that while this was true for some of the funds, others had more general uses. I assumed that half of these funds went for oil and half for discretionary purposes. I made a similar calculation for loans to Brazil under the several "bilateral cooperation agreements."

From the viewpoint of developing-country governments, including those in Latin America, loans are valuable because they usually provide resources that they themselves can control whether by the central government or SOEs. FDI is useful, but control generally rests in private hands. This situation is similar to that in the 1970s when Latin American governments sought loans from international private banks. An important difference, however, is that loans in the 1970s were deployed by Latin America's own SOEs, while most Chinese financed projects in recent years have been carried out by Chinese SOEs sometimes using imported labor.[44]

Another kind of finance going from China to Latin America is foreign aid. Aid amounts have been small in comparison to the loans just discussed (although there is some overlap), and the distribution across countries follows yet another pattern. Elsewhere, I have argued (Stallings, 2017) that China's foreign aid is basically a political tool, involving both carrot and stick. With respect to the former, it can gain friends for China's international pursuits, such as votes in international organizations on topics like human rights. And the small foreign aid loans may also help grease the wheels for larger projects financed by FDI and bank loans. At the same time, China discourages recognition of Taiwan by withholding aid from those that do not recognize the PRC, with the exception of humanitarian assistance.

According to my calculations, based on the limited Chinese data available,[45] China's foreign aid to Latin America in 2013 amounted to around US$560 million, which was 7.2 percent of total aid to the region (Stallings, 2017: 79). Excluding countries that recognized Taiwan as well as Argentina, Brazil, and Chile – which are considered too advanced to receive aid – that left nineteen countries to share the US$560 million, thus averaging about US$30 million per year. This was a relatively small amount, but sufficient to fund a number of projects desired by political leaders in recipient countries. Since Chinese aid is "demand driven," the process led to many stadiums, homes for high officials, and roads to preferred destinations.

Among the leading recipients of China's foreign aid in the region have been Cuba, Bolivia, and a number of Caribbean Islands. Cuba is a particularly interesting case. Governed by a party that is a long-time Chinese ally, it has received a large amount of aid in relative terms. Moreover, when aid resumed in the early 1990s, it came to involve support for Cuba's industrial and trade capacity. For example, China first provided Cuba with a large number of

---

[44] Kaplan (forthcoming) differentiates between loans to governments and firms.

[45] Chinese aid data, unlike FDI, are considered a state secret. Some limited data were provided in two white papers in 2011 and 2014, but they were presented at a highly aggregated level (see Stallings and Kim, 2017: chp. 4).

bicycles, then helped Cuba set up a bicycle factory. Similar policies were followed in a number of sectors. Other activities of Chinese aid involved the building of infrastructure and the development of human capital.

Bolivia has had a government with an ideological affinity toward China since the election of Evo Morales in 2005. Morales made a trip to China even before his inauguration to request help for his poverty-stricken country. He received some assistance through grants and small loans, which may have helped China in the competition for larger projects in the country. More unusual, given their political and economic characteristics, were the other main recipients of Chinese aid – the small Caribbean Islands. The GDP per capita of most of these countries is higher than China's, so it is hard to avoid the conclusion that aid to the Caribbean was mainly political. The Caribbean is where most of the Latin American countries that recognize Taiwan are located. Also, it is possible to gain many votes in international institutions for a small amount of money (Bernal, 2016).

An important contrast between trade and finance is that while trade relations between Latin America and China fell off after the boom years, capital flows actually increased. Although both FDI and loans were volatile, a clear pattern can be discerned. According to ECLAC, the post-boom period saw substantially more FDI from China than entered during the boom years. While average inflows in 2005–13 were US$6.5 billion per year, in 2014–18 they nearly doubled to US$12.2 billion. This was despite the fact that the Chinese government began to restrict outward FDI to all regions in 2017.

M&As and greenfield investments followed patterns similar to the boom period. Between 2014 and 2018, there were an annual average of ten M&A transactions versus forty-one greenfield investments; the average value per transaction was US$807 million and US$100 million, respectively. In addition to volume and type of FDI, other important changes emerged in the post-boom period. First, while the share of FDI by country remained very concentrated, with the top three countries representing 77 percent of the total, two new countries – Chile and Mexico – joined the top group. Second, manufacturing and services began to receive a larger share of investment in comparison to the earlier period when natural resources clearly dominated. And, third, although still a minority, the share of private firms increased their role in FDI to Latin America.[46]

As reported by the Inter-American Dialogue, loans from the Chinese policy banks also increased in the post-boom period, although they were slightly lower

---

[46] Data on public versus private investment are from Dussel Peters (2018). Of course, it is difficult to know exactly what a private firm is in the Chinese context; the government exerts strong control over private firms as well as SOEs.

than FDI inflows, due to a falloff in lending in 2017–18. The average annual loan inflow for the period 2005–13 was US$9.2 billion, while in 2014–18 it was US$11.7 billion. The main recipients between 2014 and 2018 were Brazil, Venezuela, Ecuador, and Argentina, which continued the trend that governments lacking access to the international capital markets turned to China as an alternative. It is notable, however, that Venezuela did not receive any new money in 2017 and only a US$5 billion credit line in 2018 to support oil production, after being the dominant borrower up to that time. Again oil and other energy investments, together with infrastructure, were the main areas of interest for China, but discretionary lending remained significant (19 percent). Within the infrastructure area, the main projects have involved buying or constructing ports. About twenty such projects are in process or have been completed since the boom ended (Myers, 2018).

In addition to loans from the two policy banks, China's four state-owned commercial banks are also becoming active in Latin America: Bank of China, China Construction Bank, Agricultural Bank of China, and Industrial and Commercial Bank of China (ICBC). In 2016, for example, ICBC provided nearly US$1 billion to Ecuador to finance government projects. In 2015, it provided a combined US$6 billion to Argentina and Brazil for a nuclear plant and iron ore projects, respectively. The Bank of China provided much smaller amounts to Ecuador (Myers and Gallagher, 2016, 2017). In addition to loans, China's commercial banks have also been setting up branches in Latin America, in part to engage in foreign exchange transactions as China seeks to have its currency used as an international means of exchange. The branches also provide services to Chinese companies and make local loans. Currently, branches are located in all of the major countries including Argentina, Brazil, Chile, Mexico, and Peru.

A new source of finance from the Chinese government, begun during the post-boom period, were three Latin American funds. The China–Latin America Cooperation Fund dates from 2014 and is capitalized at US$10–15 billion; it is managed by CHEXIM with funds from CHEXIM and the State Administration of Foreign Exchange (SAFE), the agency that handles China's international reserves. Two more funds were announced in 2015: the China–Latin America Industrial Cooperation Investment Fund (US$20 billion in capital) and the Special Loan Program for China–Latin America Infrastructure Projects (US$10 billion). Both are administered by the CDB with money from SAFE. A more specific fund was added in 2017, the US$20 billion China–Brazil Fund to concentrate on infrastructure, resource extraction, manufacturing, and agriculture (Myers and Gallagher, 2016, 2017). Unfortunately, these funds, which involve joint ventures, have quite complicated rules so that little money has actually been disbursed from them.

5.4 The Impact of the Economic Relationship with China

Of course, it is impossible to attribute economic and social trends in Latin America specifically to relations with China, but it does seem clear that the China link played a major role in the increased growth rates between 2003 and 2013.[47] Problems also resulted from those same relationships. I discuss both here briefly and then take up the more general question of dependency and the impact on development in the concluding section of the Element.

On the positive side, during the 2003–13 period, the region saw growth rates higher than for any period since the early postwar years. The average regional growth rate for 2003–13 was nearly 4 percent and investment picked up. The main ways in which China stimulated growth was through promoting exports and undertaking infrastructure projects (Dussel Peters et al., 2018). Higher growth meant that poverty declined substantially, and the labor force began to absorb new workers as well as those who had been unemployed or underemployed (see Table 4). More specific data on the employment impact of Chinese economic activities has been provided by the International Labor Organization (ILO) (Dussel Peters and Armony, 2017).[48] Their study shows that during the period 1995–2016, Chinese activities created 1.8 million (net) jobs. Nearly two-thirds resulted from trade, while FDI accounted for 15 percent and infrastructure for 20 percent. To put these figures into context, trade jobs accounted for 2.15 percent of total new employment in the region in 1995–2011. Not surprisingly, given the distribution of Chinese activities, more than half the jobs were in Brazil, while Mexico lost jobs.

In addition, the enduring inequality – which had characterized the region since the end of the nineteenth century – began to decline during the boom. A recent study by the World Bank (Messina and Silva, 2017: figure O.2) showed that both income and wage inequality in South America peaked in 2002 and fell consistently until their data end in 2012. In Mexico and Central America, which did not share the boom to the same extent that South America did, inequality also declined but not as significantly. The authors of the study attribute the

---

[47] China has what JP Morgan Global Research calls an "outsized" influence on Latin American growth. They estimate that a 1 percent growth shock by China leads to 1.4 percent growth in Latin America after four quarters (Chang, 2019). Perrotti (2015), who calculated Latin America's export elasticity to Chinese GDP, found that a 1 percent change in the latter leads to a 1.5 percent change in the former. The highest elasticity is for agricultural exports, followed by mining and industrial goods.

[48] The ILO data cover different periods (1995–2011 for trade and 2003–16 for FDI and infrastructure), and countries are limited to Argentina, Brazil, Chile, and Mexico. These four countries represented about 62 percent of the labor force in the region in 2017.

Table 4 Development trends in Latin America, 2004–18 (percent)

Year	GDP growth	Investment[a]	Exports[a]	Unemployment[b]	Poverty[c]
2004	6.3	19.1	24.7	10.4	42.6
2005	4.3	19.4	24.9	10.1	40.0
2006	5.3	20.3	24.1	9.0	35.8
2007	5.5	21.7	23.3	8.5	NA
2008	3.9	22.9	23.4	7.8	33.5
2009	−1.9	20.2	20.1	9.1	NA
2010	5.8	21.6	21.5	8.4	31.6
2011	4.4	22.1	22.7	7.7	NA
2012	2.8	22.2	21.9	7.2	28.7
2013	2.8	22.1	21.1	7.0	28.6
2014	1.0	21.2	20.3	6.9	27.8
2015	0.1	19.8	21.0	7.3	29.1
2016	−0.4	18.7	21.4	8.9	30.0
2017	1.7	18.5	21.6	9.3	30.1
2018	1.5	18.9	23.0	9.3	30.1

Sources: World Bank, *World Development Indicators* for GDP, investment, and exports; ECLAC estimates for poverty and unemployment (unpublished).
[a] share of GDP; [b] share of active population; [c] share of total population; NA is not available

decline to a number of factors: expansion of education and consequent decline in the returns to skills; increased demand for unskilled workers as growth increased and wages rose; and falling interfirm wage differences among similar workers. High growth is important, especially for the second factor.

On the less positive side, growth cycles continued. As the China Boom ended, growth in the region became sluggish at best. Between 2014 and 2018, GDP aggregate growth averaged only 0.8 percent with negative growth in 2016. Of course, the low aggregate growth rate implied a negative rate for per capita GDP (−0.2 percent). Likewise, open (urban) unemployment rose from a low of 6.9 percent in 2014 to 9.3 percent in 2018, and underemployment increased. Poverty followed a similar path with a low in 2014 of 27.8 percent of the population below the poverty line and 7.8 percent in extreme poverty; by 2018, the rate had risen to 30.1 and 10.7 percent, respectively. In absolute terms, the period 2014–18 saw an increase of more than 20 million more people in poverty. (For recent discussions of unemployment and poverty, see ECLAC, 2019a and 2019b).

The renewed emphasis on natural resource extraction also implies serious problems for future development. One is the volatility intrinsic to this sector. Another is a backtracking on employment gains, since natural resource extraction is generally capital intensive with few links with the rest of the economy. An important example concerns Chile, where a Chinese company purchased a 24 percent stake in the main Chilean lithium company, as part of its strategy for vertical integration in the electric vehicle industry. It appears that China will push the company to export raw lithium to China rather than produce batteries in Chile. Indeed, Chile's relations with China have generally pushed it back in the value added of its raw materials exports (Luksic, 2019). At the same time, the region's industrial sector has been undermined by competition from Chinese products with their advantage in cheap labor and credit. The most serious example is Mexico, which has been priced out of the US market in many products, but even Brazil has had problems in protecting its domestic market from cheap Chinese goods. Thus, Brazil has been particularly active in bringing anti-dumping cases against China in the WTO. In the infrastructure sector, problems have arisen with respect to quality (e.g., in Ecuador), but concern is also expressed over the types of projects in which China is particularly interested. Most prominent is investment in ports, which could increase Chinese leverage with local governments and potentially be dual-use facilities (Myers, 2018).

In addition, Chinese investment at home and abroad, including in Latin America, has been associated with lack of attention to the environmental implications of natural resources extraction and export agriculture.[49] Some Chinese firms have followed best practices, but in general they lack the experience or the desire to do so. A recent study of the topic (Ray et al., 2017: chp. 1) finds that Latin American exports to China cause more greenhouse gas emissions and use more water per dollar of output than exports to the rest of the world or than Latin America's overall production. Part of the greenhouse gas problem is due to deforestation, which also has negative impacts on biodiversity. Finally, despite the rhetoric of South–South cooperation and mutual benefit, China has not offered significant assistance in two areas of crucial importance to Latin America – increasing the value added of its exports and making investments in China. I have personally asked many Chinese officials about these issues, but the answers are generally the same: these problems are up to Latin America to deal with.[50]

---

[49] Economy (2018: 182–3) discusses China's general willingness to export its environmental problems to developing countries.

[50] See Inter-American Development Bank (2014) on problems for Latin American investment in China.

6 China–Latin America Political Relations

The common view is that China's relations with developing countries, including Latin America, are all about economics. While economic relations are definitely dominant, and while China's mantra of noninterference in the internal affairs of other nations would seem to downplay the role of politics, it is nonetheless important to examine political relations on their own since they have an autonomous role. Political relations can be divided into four categories: multilateral diplomacy, bilateral diplomacy, person-to-person diplomacy, and security/military relations.

As seen in Section 3, US political relations with Latin America often involved leverage, including the use of military force and clandestine operations as well as economic pressure on host governments to give privileges to US corporations. Chinese political relations with Southeast Asia also feature leverage, but those with Latin America have been different – at least up to the present. Rather than political leverage, China has sought to use linkage-type relationships, such as presidential visits, the establishment of institutions to tie China and Latin America, promises of aid and investment, and cultural and educational exchanges. The narrative of South–South cooperation is emblematic of the Chinese approach.

The broader question concerns the long-term relationship between economics and politics. Is there a strict separation between the two, such that China's economic relations are based on commercial considerations with its political relations the purview of foreign policy officials? Or are both part of a grand strategy that would tie developing countries, including Latin America, into China's vision of a dominant international role for itself? It is impossible to answer this question in a definitive way, but the fact that trade and financial relations are mostly carried out by SOEs lends credence to the second formulation. Also, some investments, especially in ports, can have political implications as well as economic ones. At a minimum, as we will see, the Chinese government has used political tools in the last few years to try to offset economic problems that Latin Americans perceive as deriving from a decline in Chinese imports from the region.

I begin this section by setting up a political baseline, focusing on diplomatic relations before the 2000s (including the Taiwan issue) and Chinese immigration to the region. I then examine multilateral diplomacy through the Chinese Foreign Ministry's two white papers on Latin America, presidential visits to the region, and the establishment of new regional institutions to facilitate China–Latin America relations together with membership in existing regional institutions. Bilateral diplomacy is necessary for the larger countries in the region, both to strengthen ongoing relations and to deal with problems that arise. A complementary topic is person-to-person diplomacy through educational and cultural activities. I conclude with a brief discussion of military and security relations, a topic not usually included in the literature, but which may become more important in the future.

6.1 China-Latin America Political Relations Before 2000

One of the earliest ways in which China and Latin America met was through Chinese emigration to the region. The main emigration flow was the so-called coolie trade in the nineteenth century, when unskilled laborers from Southern China left to seek economic opportunities in Cuba and Peru, but also in Mexico, Argentina, and Central America (Look Lai, 2010). Chinese immigrants arrived in the twentieth century as a result of the communist victory on the mainland and the PRC takeover of Hong Kong and Macao. Thus, while a Chinese presence exists in a number of countries, Chinese immigrants do not form a cohesive community akin to their Japanese counterparts, so China has not been able to take advantage of the diaspora in Latin America as much as it has in Asia and elsewhere.

Another set of interactions that preceded the current period involved diplomatic recognition of China. For the first decade after the establishment of the PRC government, all Latin American governments recognized Taiwan. Cuba was the first Latin American country to establish diplomatic relations with the PRC, in 1960, after the advent of the Castro regime. Recognition was rewarded by various types of Chinese aid – including food, weapons, and training programs. After a break when Cuba sided with the Soviet Union in the Sino–Soviet disputes, China and Cuba again became close allies. Ten years after Cuba's diplomatic initiative and soon after Salvador Allende was elected president on a socialist ticket, Chile became the first South American country to recognize the PRC. Again, Chinese aid followed, including food, a long-term loan, and cash assistance following a natural disaster.[51]

During the 1970s and 1980s, following the US lead, all major Latin American nations established diplomatic relations with China, although a substantial number of smaller countries continued to recognize Taiwan. The competition between the PRC and Taiwan for the allegiance of Latin America has been an important issue in the history of China's foreign aid and other types of relations in the region. Over half of the countries that still recognize Taiwan are in Latin America, mostly in Central America and the Caribbean. Since eliminating

---

[51] China and Romania were the only socialist countries that maintained relations with Chile's military government; Pinochet appeared to get on well with the PRC (see Anderson, 1998).

Taiwan's relations with the rest of the world is a major PRC foreign policy goal, it has been very generous with countries that have switched their allegiance. A shift was started by Dominica (2004), Grenada (2005), and Costa Rica (2007), followed a decade later by Panama (2017), the Dominican Republic (2018), and El Salvador (2018). These changes leave fifteen countries that recognize Taiwan, of which nine are in Latin America.[52]

6.2 Multilateral Diplomacy

The Chinese Ministry of Foreign Affairs has issued two white papers on Latin America and the Caribbean since the boom began. The first came out in 2008, and the second appeared in 2016 (People's Republic of China, Ministry of Foreign Affairs, 2008, 2016). The two cover similar themes with respect to economics, but the second one was more detailed and added some new topics. Both papers are filled with diplomatic boilerplate, as seen in the preamble of the first:

> The Chinese Government views its relations with Latin America and the Caribbean from a strategic plane and seeks to build and develop a comprehensive and cooperative partnership featuring equality, mutual benefit and common development with Latin American and Caribbean countries. The goals of China's policy on Latin America and the Caribbean are: promote mutual respect and mutual trust and expand common ground; deepen cooperation and achieve win-win results; draw on each other's strengths to boost common progress and intensify exchanges; and the one China principle is the political basis for the establishment and development of relations between China and Latin American and Caribbean countries and regional organizations.

A slightly greater level of specificity was found in the agenda itself, but the thirty-five items mentioned were also extremely general. In the political field: high-level exchanges, exchanges between legislatures, exchanges between political parties, consultation mechanisms, cooperation in international affairs, and local government exchanges. With respect to economics: trade, investment cooperation, financial cooperation, agricultural cooperation, industrial cooperation, infrastructure construction, resources and energy cooperation, cooperation on quality inspection, tourism cooperation, debt reduction and cancellation, economic and technical assistance, multilateral cooperation, and chamber of commerce cooperation. On cultural and social aspects: cultural and sports exchanges; cooperation in science, technology, and education; cooperation in

---

[52] On reasons for the ten-year gap between Costa Rica and Panama in recognizing the PRC, see Parajon (2019).

medical and health care; consular cooperation and personnel exchanges; media cooperation; people-to-people exchanges; cooperation in environmental protection; cooperation in combating climate change; cooperation in human resources and social security; disaster reduction, disaster relief, and humanitarian assistance; and cooperation in poverty reduction. On peace, security, and judicial affairs: military exchanges and cooperation, cooperation in judicial and police affairs, and nontraditional security issues.

It is hard to get a sense of priorities from this document – although clearly the dominant theme is cooperation. The word "cooperation" is mentioned in the heading of about half the items and discussed in the four or five lines of content for each item if not included in the heading itself. Nonetheless, there is little indication of what cooperation would involve in practice. The second white paper was released during President Xi's appearance at the Asia-Pacific Economic Cooperation (APEC) summit in Lima in November 2016. Similar to the first one, it did add some new topics (space and maritime cooperation) and provided more detail about cooperation between the two sides. In the intervening years, China had learned more about Latin America, but lack of knowledge and understanding on both sides remains a significant hindrance to closer relations.

Another show of interest in the region involves visits by high-level Chinese officials. Since 2000, Chinese presidents have visited Latin America ten times. While President Xi's visits to individual Latin American countries have been combined with attendance at international meetings held in the region, his predecessors came to the region specifically to meet with Latin American leaders. They included two trips by Jiang Zemin: a twelve-day visit to six countries (Argentina, Brazil, Chile, Cuba, Uruguay, and Venezuela) in 2001 and a stop in Mexico in 2002. They also included four trips by Hu Jintao: to Argentina, Brazil, Chile, and Cuba in 2004; to Mexico in 2005; to Costa Rica, Cuba, and Panama in 2008; and to Brazil in 2010. Finally, Xi Jinping has made four trips as president, as discussed later. This type of presidential trip by Chinese leaders is filled with symbolism and promises about economic relations in addition to declarations of friendship. For example, during Hu's trip in 2004, he announced US$100 billion of Chinese investment in the region over the ensuing ten years as well as US$100 billion in trade.[53] Needless to say, almost all Latin American presidents also made visits to China.

President Xi's multiple visits to Latin America between 2013 and 2018 took place within the context of souring relations with the region. Given the

---

[53] There were doubts about these numbers, especially about the investment, and some Chinese experts thought the translation was mixed up (see Stallings, 2008: 250).

recession that hit Latin America in the years after the boom ended in 2013, there was a tendency to blame the bad times on China. For example, the Pew Global Attitudes Survey indicated that between 2013 and 2017, opinion about China fell in terms of net favorability in the five largest countries of the region (except for Mexico).[54] Consequently, it would appear that Chinese officials were looking to counteract adverse economic trends. As we have already seen, FDI and loans were increased; the government had significant control over these flows. But direct political steps were also taken, including four presidential visits in the space of six years.

In June 2013, shortly after assuming office as president of China, Xi visited Mexico, Costa Rica, and Trinidad and Tobago. In Mexico, he tried to improve relations that were strained because of Mexico's disadvantageous economic position with regard to China. In Costa Rica, he initiated large-scale infrastructure projects in collaboration with China's new FTA partner, and in Trinidad and Tobago he met with eight Caribbean leaders. More significant was Xi's ten-day journey to the region in July 2014. That trip combined a BRICS (Brazil, Russia, India, China, and South Africa) Leaders' Meeting in Brazil, with bilateral meetings in Brazil, Argentina, Venezuela, and Cuba, where multiple agreements were signed.

President Xi's third trip to Latin America was to attend the APEC Leaders' Meeting in Lima in November 2016, which he combined with state visits to Peru and Chile as well as a trip to Ecuador. In each of his three stops, he signed agreements on economic activities and joint projects; all involved some diversification away from the traditional Chinese emphasis on natural resources. Finally, President Xi attended the G20 meeting in Buenos Aires in November/ December 2018. The G20 was followed by Xi's second state visit to host country, Argentina, and then he proceeded to Panama, one of the countries that recently switched its allegiance to the PRC. Panama has been very aggressive in pursuing the new relationship. A score of agreements were signed, and negotiations were started for what would be Latin America's fourth FTA with China.

Supplementing and complementing presidential visits and those of other high officials were activities of regional institutions. The most significant institution is the China–CELAC Forum,[55] which the Chinese have tried to make the premier organization linking the two regions. At the meeting in Brasilia in

---

[54] Net favorability means favorable minus unfavorable attitudes. The Mexico case seems to have been a reaction against President Trump's stand on Mexico; opinion about the United States fell as that of China rose (Walz, 2018).

[55] CELAC is the Community of Latin American and Caribbean States, an organization of all countries in the Western Hemisphere except the United States and Canada.

2014 that established the forum, Xi hinted at broadening Chinese economic activities from natural resources to other sectors including energy, infrastructure, agriculture, manufacturing, science and technology, and information technology. The ambitious goals to be attained were US$500 billion in trade and US $250 billion in investment over the next ten years (People's Republic of China, Ministry of Foreign Affairs, 2014).

A first ministerial summit of the China–CELAC Forum was held in Beijing in 2015 and a second in Santiago, Chile, in 2018. At the Santiago meeting, in addition to the usual declaration promising friendship and cooperation, an action plan was approved for the period from 2019 until 2021, when the third meeting will be held in China. It called for activities in the politics and security area, economics, science and technology, the environment, and cultural exchanges. Potentially most interesting, but also conflictive, was a declaration that dealt with the BRI. China promoted the BRI and invited Latin American and Caribbean countries to join. CELAC ministers "welcomed with interest the presentation of the Chinese Foreign Minister," but no commitments were made. While some countries were enthusiastic, others were more suspicious, and no joint decision was forthcoming. Later, however, a number of individual countries have become affiliated with the BRI.[56]

China has also pursued affiliation with a number of existing regional organizations. A first example was its acceptance in 2004 to be a permanent observer at the Organization of American States (OAS). Other regional institutions where China is an observer include the Latin American Integration Association (LAIA), the Latin American Parliament, and the Pacific Alliance. A more significant undertaking was China's acceptance in 2008 as a member of the IDB. As a donor member of the IDB, China agreed to contribute US$350 million for programs including soft loans to the poorest Latin American countries, support for an equity fund to be administered by the Inter-American Investment Corporation, and money for the Multilateral Investment Fund that lends to microenterprises.

6.3 Bilateral Diplomacy

While China pursues relations with the Latin American region as a whole, bilateral relations are still of the utmost importance, especially with respect to the major countries in the region. Dealing with the Caribbean countries as a group can be acceptable, but the larger countries require individual treatment,

---

[56] Eighteen countries have signed memoranda of understanding with BRI – although the significance of these documents is not clear. Many of the BRI countries are traditional Chinese allies; others are small Caribbean nations. Chile, Costa Rica, and Uruguay have also joined. A recent analysis of the BRI and Latin America is Zhang (2019).

particularly when problems exist between the two sides. Realization of the need for bilateral diplomacy is on display in the visits to individual countries of which the largest number have involved Argentina, Brazil, Chile, Cuba, and Mexico. China has different categories of relationships within the region, as elsewhere. The top seven countries, which China calls "comprehensive strategic partners," are Argentina, Brazil, Chile, Ecuador, Mexico, Peru, and Venezuela. Three other countries – Bolivia, Costa Rica, and Uruguay – are "strategic partners."[57] Among countries recognizing China, the only major one left out is Colombia. Others are small countries and/or recent diplomatic partners of the PRC. Cuba is a special case, since relations between the two countries are managed by their respective communist parties.

Several Latin American countries have been of particular concern to China in recent years. The most obvious is Venezuela, which has received more money from China than any other country in the region. As an indication of China's need to import petroleum, but also perhaps of its greater astuteness in comparison to the West, China linked Venezuelan loans to repayment in oil. Consequently, while both Chinese banks and US bondholders lent Venezuela about US$60 billion, Venezuela's debt to US lenders is still that amount, while its outstanding debt to China is only about US$20 billion. Nonetheless, the Chinese want to get their expected returns on their investment and have struggled to find a way to deal with Venezuela.[58]

China–Venezuela relations began in the early 2000s when Hugo Chávez decided to court the Asian giant to help reduce his reliance on the United States. While China refused to get involved in Chávez's political battles, it was willing to finance him under certain conditions. In 2007, CDB began supporting Venezuela's oil investments through a China–Venezuela investment fund. This financing was in exchange for two conditions: repayment via delivery of future Venezuelan oil shipments and guaranteed contracts for Chinese companies. The loans burgeoned after the financial crisis, enabling Chávez to continue his massive social programs in the face of falling oil prices.

As long as Chávez was president, he could hold together Venezuela's economy to a minimal degree. His successor, Nicolás Maduro, had far greater difficulties and came to rely on China even more. Loans kept coming until the end of 2016. The Chinese seem unsure about what to do. Their main client in Latin America has an economy and a political system in chaos; moreover,

---

[57] The significance of these (and other) categories of diplomatic relations is opaque. The main English-language source of information on them is found in works by Chinese scholars (Feng and Huang, 2014 and Xu, 2017).

[58] A recent analysis of economic relations between China and Venezuela is Kaplan and Penfold (2019).

Venezuela's oil production is plunging so it cannot keep up with payments on its loans. In September 2018, Maduro visited China and received a US$5 billion credit line to support oil production. The Venezuela disaster has tarnished China's reputation internationally, and the government fears that it will arouse political protests at home if Venezuela were to default on its loans.[59]

The other kind of bilateral problem that has worried Beijing in the past few years is of a quite different sort – although it might come to pass in Venezuela later on. That is, a number of leftist governments to whom China had made extensive commitments via loans and/or FDI were replaced by more conservative governments in Argentina, Brazil, Ecuador, and Peru.[60] The earliest case was Argentina, when Mauricio Macri replaced Cristina Kirchner in 2015. Since money going to Argentina, like that in many cases, had been negotiated with little transparency, Chinese officials feared that Macri would refuse to honor the agreements. Indeed, he indicated that he would review the loans, but ultimately decided to go along and even obtained modest additional amounts of Chinese finance for small and medium-sized enterprise development, railway modernization, and solar projects (Patey, 2017).

In Ecuador, leftist economist and president, Rafael Correa, began borrowing from China after the country's debt default in 2008. By the time Correa left office in mid-2017, Ecuador had received over US$17 billion from CDB and CHEXIM. Most went for hydroelectric projects, which have caused notorious problems in the country (Casey and Krauss, 2018). These loans were also backed by the country's petroleum exports. While Ecuador's economic problems do not approach those of Venezuela, payments to China are eating up at least half of its oil revenues and on increasingly onerous terms as oil prices have fallen. Thus, new president, Lenín Moreno, broke with his former mentor (Correa) and sought to renegotiate the loan terms with China. Those negotiations are ongoing.

Finally, the elephant in the room at the moment is Brazil. Brazil has the deepest relationship with China of any country in the region. The earliest strategic partner, it has the largest trade links and has received substantial amounts of foreign capital (mainly in oil, mining, and energy). Nonetheless, the recently elected president of Brazil, Jair Bolsonaro, was highly critical of

---

[59] It is interesting to contrast China's reaction to the situation in Venezuela with that in Sri Lanka. In the latter case, China took control of a port and surrounding territory when the government could not keep up loan payments. Of course, Sri Lanka is a smaller country, but it also seems to be an example of China's different treatment of Asian and Latin American countries.

[60] Chile and Colombia also saw electoral shifts to the right, but fewer Chinese investments had been made in those countries.

China during the campaign. "The Chinese are not buying in Brazil. They are buying Brazil" was a favorite slogan (Spring, 2018). Obviously, the Chinese government and the companies involved are concerned as to whether Bolsonaro will change his approach, as Macri did, or whether he will try to make significant changes in the relationship. Recent interactions, including visits to Beijing by Brazil's vice president and by Bolsonaro himself, indicate a pragmatic approach.

6.4 Person-to-Person Diplomacy

While all of these initiatives are examples of China's use of linkage in order to strengthen relations with governments of the region, other activities focus on individuals. The Chinese understand that they need allies at all levels. While government leaders are most important, allies in educational institutions, the media, and civil society organizations are also useful. This realization was made clear in the white papers, where exchanges were mentioned frequently.

A typical activity is offering scholarships to study in China. These include both special courses to promote technical skills as well as the opportunity to study at major Chinese universities. Indeed, most Chinese universities now have MA programs specifically geared for students from developing countries who get degrees in international studies or sometimes in Chinese studies (Li and Yang, 2018). Education has been an important topic in all presidential visits to the region. During President Xi's 2016 speech at the APEC summit, he promised to provide scholarships for at least 10,000 students per year to study in China.

If educational exchanges are typical of all countries seeking to influence others, China's Confucius Institutes are unique. Run by the Ministry of Education, these centers operate all over the world, including in the United States, Europe, and other parts of Asia. Currently, in Latin America, there are thirty-nine Confucius Institutes in twenty countries. A key role is to teach the Chinese language, with some 100,000 students enrolled (National Endowment for Democracy, 2017). The Confucius Institutes are a major example of China's use of linkage, and many of the leading universities in Latin America have agreed to host them. In addition, a regional center was set up in Santiago, one of only three in the world. At the China–CELAC Forum meeting in Santiago in January 2018, a gathering of people from the various individual institutes was held.[61]

---

[61] A strong critique of the Confucius Institutes was recently published by the National Endowment for Democracy (2017). The authors refer to China's soft power as "sharp power."

6.5 Security and Military Relations

The least known aspect of Chinese relations with Latin America is security and military relations. Both of the Chinese white papers mentioned the desirability of greater military cooperation, and some US politicians have expressed great concern about the security implications of a Chinese presence in the hemisphere. While the actual security-related activities – as opposed to economic and political relations that might have security implications – are not very extensive at this time, they do exist and are expanding.[62]

Military exchanges are similar in some ways to educational and other cultural exchanges. The number of visits to Latin America by senior Chinese defense officials, and the number of visits to China by their counterparts, have increased over past years. The most frequent exchanges are with those countries in the region that are openly anti-American and so cannot buy equipment from the United States – Venezuela, Bolivia, Ecuador (under Correa), Argentina (under the Kirchners), and Nicaragua. The exchanges occur both at a high level (ministers and heads of military operations) and at lower levels. In the case of the former, they may involve not only exchanges of view, but also agreements for arms purchases or joint activities.

Institutional activities are also important. For example, the People's Liberation Army (PLA) spent eight years (2004–12) participating in the UN Peacekeeping Force in Haiti. In the process, it made extensive contacts with Latin American militaries and got first-hand experience operating in a Latin American environment. Another set of institutional activities involves the PLA's National Defense University, which has several units that offer courses in English and Spanish for Latin American officers. A number of ongoing exchanges of an institutional sort involve countries that are not politically aligned with China. Chile, Argentina, Colombia, and Peru are examples of regular exchanges that occur in both directions. An important conference took place in October 2015, when China's Defense Ministry hosted officers from eleven Latin American countries for a ten-day forum on military logistics (Londono, 2018).

Military sales are another aspect of security relations between China and Latin America. China's worldwide arms exports have increased substantially. Between 2001 and 2016, Latin America accounted for 6 percent of arms outflows from China (Gurrola, 2018). Most of them involved Venezuela, Bolivia, and Ecuador; Venezuela's Chávez was instrumental in introducing Chinese

---

[62] The main expert on China–Latin America security relations is R. Evan Ellis from the US Army War College Strategic Studies Institute. This section draws from Ellis (2013, 2018). See also Piccone (2016) and Koleski and Blivas (2018).

arms merchants to his counterparts in friendly countries in the region. Many arms transactions began as donations or small purchases of nonlethal items, but they have increased in value and sophistication. Venezuela, the largest client, has purchased fighter planes as well as transport aircraft, helicopters, and radar equipment. Bolivia has bought military aircraft from China as well as cargo and passenger planes and helicopters. Ecuador bought radar and surveillance equipment. At the same time, China has encountered problems in its attempts to sell military equipment in the region, especially to countries beyond the small group of its closest allies. In addition to quality, maintenance is an issue since China does not have facilities in the region.

The project that has aroused most opposition is the Argentine space station in Patagonia, which was negotiated by Cristina Kirchner. It is a US$50 million operation that is part of China's exploration of the far side of the moon; the Argentine site is a tracking station. China was given the land, rent free, for fifty years in return for undisclosed promises of benefits. One reason that many Argentines and others have objected is that the project was negotiated in secret by a government that was desperate for foreign exchange. There are also concerns that it could enhance China's intelligence-gathering capabilities in the Western Hemisphere (Londono, 2018).

All of these types of political relationships represent attempts by China to use linkage methods in its interactions with Latin America governments, firms, and citizens. China has substituted linkage for the use of political leverage, a more common mechanism in United States–Latin America relations and of Chinese relations with its Southeast Asian neighbors. As to why the difference exists, my hypothesis is that it involves three factors. First, the geographical distance between China and Latin America makes the use of force more difficult than in nearby areas. Second, the lack of knowledge about Latin America, including both its political structure and its cultural norms, inhibits an aggressive stance. Third, and perhaps most important, the continuing presence of the United States in the region – in economic as well as political terms – gives China the incentive to adopt a relatively low profile to avoid antagonizing what is still the dominant country in the world.

7 On Dependency

This Element has covered many years and a considerable part of the globe in search of an answer as to whether the concept of dependency is helpful in understanding the process of development. Since the concept arose in and about Latin America, I started there and examined Latin America's relationships with the United States in the twentieth century in light of the legacy of its earlier ties with Spain, Portugal, and Britain. Next I looked halfway around the world to imperial China and its history both in dominating its neighbors over millennia and then, for a brief century, under the domination of Europe and Japan. Finally, I joined these two discussions and asked about China's relations with Latin America in the twenty-first century.

This concluding section has two parts. The first looks at the question of whether China's relations with Latin America are usefully portrayed as relations of dependency. This question can be addressed in comparison with the earlier analysis of China's links with Southeast Asia and sub-Saharan Africa. A companion question is whether such relations have had major implications for the development process in the region. The second part expands that discussion to ask if the concept of dependency is worth preserving more generally – despite the heavy criticism it has received from many quarters.

My answers to all of these questions are in the affirmative. In reverse order, I argue that it is impossible to adequately analyze the development process anywhere without taking the systemic context into account. In the long run, this includes analyzing how a given country was incorporated into the international system; in the short run, it focuses on the characteristics of the hegemonic country(ies) and the mechanisms through which they influence peripheral or semi-peripheral countries. In no way does this imply that internal factors are not important, but external forces must be an important part of the analysis. The crucial task, as Fernando Henrique Cardoso told us decades ago, is to study how the internal and the external interact. Going further, I also argue that the external context has often had a negative impact on development in periods up to the present, without denying the existence of dependent development, and those domestic and international factors that drive it, as defined by those who have embraced the term. Nonetheless, as Cardoso and colleagues themselves admit, dependent development is not a sufficient goal in and of itself. In particular, it omits the crucial question of how to incorporate a larger share of the population into the benefits of growth and progress.

China's rise on the world stage, I argue, is creating significant changes in the way the international system operates and the nature of center-peripheral relations. It is opening up new opportunities for developing countries, but it is also imposing new constraints. China's own needs, especially for raw materials, involve it in relations that can be harmful to its partners. Enticing them back to natural resource extraction as the engine of growth – with little concern for labor or environmental rights – cannot be offset by the advantages of markets and finance that are the quid pro quo. This is particularly the case with Southeast Asia and Africa, where China faces less competition and weak governments, enabling it to take a heavy-handed approach. In Latin America up until now,

China has operated in a more hands-off way, arguably in part because of the traditional hegemonic role of the United States in the region. Nonetheless, there are some similarities between Latin America and the other developing regions that may be harbingers of the future.

7.1 Dependency Involving China and Latin America

To tackle the specific question of how to conceptualize China's relations with Latin America, I again use the mechanisms introduced in Section 2 of markets, leverage, and linkage. I take it for granted that the exact forms of markets, leverage, and linkage have changed significantly over time and place. But, of course, there must be recognizable similarities, despite these changes, for the use of these categories to make sense. My argument is that those similarities exist and that we can gain traction by employing the three mechanisms to help understand China's relationships in the region. One way of thinking about these changes is to return to the Cardoso–Faletto idea of "situations of dependency." Those situations vary according to internal characteristics of dependent countries, but also according to characteristics of the hegemon.

As seen in Table 3, dependency in the case of China and Southeast Asia/sub-Saharan Africa has relied more on leverage than on markets or on linkage. In the case of the United States and Latin America (Table 1), markets were especially important and leverage and linkage were about equally relevant. These differences have to do with the respective characteristics of the United States and China. Markets are more important in a capitalist economy than in a state capitalist one, despite China's greater openness to markets after Deng Xiaoping's reforms. Also, China's long history of authoritarian rule with respect to its neighbors – and its own population – has left the government less concerned to seek voluntary cooperation and consensus through linkage mechanisms. But how does this play out in the Latin American context, where relations with China may present other situations of dependency?

Table 5 aims to help answer this question. It divides the Latin American experience with China into three categories. Latin America-1 represents countries that have been willing to accept China's rules. These countries – Venezuela, Bolivia, Ecuador under Correa, Argentina under the Kirchners, and perhaps Peru under Humala – bear resemblance to the pattern discussed for Southeast Asia and Africa. Their willingness to sign contracts in backrooms left them at the mercy of China's economic leverage in spite of the market context. This power was reinforced for those governments with respect to finance, since they had little access to international capital markets and so China assumed an especially important role. Trade relationships, which often

Table 5 Dependency involving China and Latin America, 2003–18

	Latin America-1	Latin America-2	
	2003–18	2003–13	2014–18
Markets	Low	Medium	Medium
Leverage	Medium (Economic)	Low	Low
Linkage	Low	Low	Medium

For definitions of Latin America-1 and -2, see text.

involved countries' major export products pledged to repay loans, were another example of the interrelationship between markets and leverage. In this situation, linkage was less important because government officials already identified with the Chinese perspective (e.g., Chávez and Morales) or did not care about it.

For other countries in the region, by contrast, the dependency mechanisms look different; these are the portrayed in Table 5 under the Latin America-2 headings. These are countries that pride themselves on following transparent rules and international standards of governance. Examples include Chile, Colombia, Costa Rica, Mexico, Uruguay, and Brazil most of the time. Since these countries do not need China as much as their counterparts just discussed, they have more power in negotiating the rules of the game. Of particular importance is an open bidding process for government procurement and infrastructure projects as well as trade contracts that are openly negotiated and based on international prices.[63] In these circumstances, markets become more important and leverage less so. At no time, in either set of Latin American countries, have the Chinese engaged in the forcible actions seen in the United States–Latin America relationships in the postwar period or in China's relations with Southeast Asia. Even in the case of Venezuela, China has taken a low-profile stance in comparison with the leverage exerted by Russia.

In the absence of leverage, the relevance of linkage has increased during recent years. As economic performance in Latin America deteriorated after the boom ended, with some tendency to blame China for the recession, China began to increase its political activities in the region. Examples included presidential attention in the form of lengthy visits; institutions such as the new China–CELAC Forum, which offered cooperation in various areas; and educational opportunities including both scholarships for Latin American students to study

---

[63] A similar analysis is found in Kaplan (forthcoming). Kaplan presents a quantitative measure of the differences across groups of countries in Latin America.

in China and the Confucius Institutes locally. The fostering of FTAs was as much about linkage as about markets in this context. Whether such activities have reconciled Latin American governments and citizens to more extensive interactions with China, and what the rules of engagement should be, remains to be seen. Debate on policy toward China is ongoing at present.

How have these relations of dependency impacted the development process in Latin America? By the time China arrived on the scene in a significant way, there were already countries that had crossed the dependent development threshold. If dependent development implied a strong, internationally competitive industrial sector, then Brazil and Mexico were the main examples. If it is broader in terms of institutional capacity to manage an economy efficiently, then Chile, Colombia, Costa Rica, Uruguay, and increasingly Peru would also qualify. Two questions then arise. Did relations with China promote further dependent development? And did they facilitate a broader definition of development that would include social services, poverty reduction, and greater equality?

My basic answer to both questions is negative: relations with China have undermined dependent development and done nothing to help promote inclusive development. What China did was to provide markets and finance that led to relatively high rates of growth for a time. But the quality of that growth was problematic. The overwhelming emphasis on natural resource exports in South America, and the inability to compete with China's industrial exports throughout the region, have undermined the industries that had been so painstakingly constructed over more than a century and subjected the countries to volatile growth because of price fluctuations for commodities. Moving back to natural resources had negative implications for employment – as the sector is generally capital-intensive – and productivity growth. It also has had negative implications for the environment. At the same time, China has been unwilling to support Latin American countries in the main area of interest to the region – increasing the value-added of their production and especially their exports. Nor has it offered much assistance to Latin American firms wanting to invest in China.

As a counterpoint, China has been helping with the building of infrastructure in the region, the lack of which poses a serious impediment to development today. But more attention needs to be focused on the construction process, including the use of Chinese companies and labor, and on the routes taken by the projects. To take one prominent example, China proposed to finance and build a transcontinental railroad that would lower costs for transporting goods from Brazil to China. It was to pass through parts of the Amazon that have delicate environmental ecosystems, but the Chinese were not particularly concerned.

The project is currently on hold because of disputes between the various parties, including civil society protests in the two countries (Drout, 2018).

In terms of inclusive growth, higher growth rates were certainly helpful during the boom. Unemployment and poverty fell, and growth was probably a factor in declining inequality. But the volatility that has always characterized raw material exports reemerged with the downturn after 2013, and the social gains of the previous decade began to disappear. These trends can be seen by looking back at Table 4. A crucial question is whether the post-2013 period is just a short-term cyclical phenomenon or whether it is part of China's "new normal."

As one of the leading observers of the China–Latin America relationship reminds us (Gallagher, 2016), it behooves Latin American governments and private-sector actors alike to think about the implications of the new normal and about the China relationship in general. A key requirement for a better relationship is less passivity vis-à-vis China. This relates both to a strategy for dealing with China on an individual country basis and more regional cooperation in carrying out such a strategy. China is not to blame for the current situation in the region; it is merely following its own self-interest. Latin American countries have to figure out what their interests are and how to implement them as Cardoso and Faletto told us. Barring that, the negative impact of dependency relations will persist.

7.2 The Usefulness of Dependency Analysis

Finally, what about the more general usefulness (or not) of the concept of dependency? With respect to this question, I find an article by Herman Schwartz (2007) on "Dependency or Institutions?" to be particularly helpful. Schwartz carries out his discussion in the abstract terms of "unit-level explanations" and "system-level explanations," and he also asks a very broad question – what explains the global distribution of growth and economic activity? Nevertheless, his analysis touches on many of the same concerns discussed in this Element.

He critiques three logical deficiencies of unit-level explanations: the assumption that all system-level explanations are wrong because of weaknesses in some; the assumption that all system-level explanations are stated in absolute (as opposed to probabilistic) terms, which leaves them open to simple disconfirmation by example; and failure to recognize that system-level variables may account for the existence of unit-level relationships. His criticism of system-level arguments is the "lack of precisely specified causal mechanisms" (p. 119), including the lack of microfoundations. He points to economic geography in the work of von Thunen (1966) and Krugman (1991) as examples of the way out of this criticism by "provid[ing] simple and plausible mechanisms for the four core claims of most system-level arguments – conditioning of peripheral economies, the inseparability of development and underdevelopment, the persistence of underdevelopment, and core-periphery linkages" (p. 132). My approach, as discussed in previous sections, is to focus on the markets/leverage/linkage triad of mechanisms to cast light on specific trends and relationships in the center-periphery context.

In order to avoid a "barren dialogue," Schwartz calls for integrating the two types of analysis. This need to integrate system and unit-level analysis – which I call international and domestic analysis – has long been a concern of the best of the dependency analysts. The idea that it is possible to understand the development process in Latin America, or anywhere else for that matter, by looking only at internal factors and relationships is pure folly. In economic texts, authors start with a closed economy model, but realize that relaxing closed-economy constraints is necessary if understanding the real world is the goal. But it would be equally foolish to argue that everything that happens in developing countries can be explained from the outside. The differences among development experiences, even within Latin America itself, constitute prima facie evidence that this is not the case. The key is to understand the interrelationships.

At the systems level, the vastly increased role of China is obviously changing how the system operates. It provides the opportunity for developing countries in some regions, including Latin America, to diversify their relations within the international system, but that depends on China not becoming completely dominant. In part, it is up to the developing countries themselves to keep their options open, but the willingness of core countries to stay in the game is also essential. The current tendency of the United States to pull back from its international commitments, and even its regional commitments, is troubling. Developing countries everywhere should search for as many partners as possible. The announced desire on the part of several Southeast Asian countries to maintain, or even expand, their relationships with the United States as a counter to China is but one example. In addition, of course, developing countries must strengthen their own institutions and policies to put them in a more favorable situation when it comes to dealing with China and other core countries.

Whether we use the term "dependency" or not is of little relevance – although the habit of each author trying to invent a new term for an old phenomenon is not helpful. What is important is that we recognize and analyze the ways in which external economic and political phenomena play a crucial role in explaining decisions of public and private actors and the outcomes of those decisions in terms of development in Latin America and elsewhere.

References

Abbott, J. P. (2003). *Developmentalism and Dependency in Southeast Asia: The Case of the Automotive Industry*. London: Routledge.

Abi-Habib, M. (2018). How China Got Sri Lanka to Cough Up a Port. *New York Times*, June 25.

Agbebi, M., and P. Virtanen (2017). Dependency Theory – A Conceptual Lens to Understand China's Presence in Africa? *Forum for Development Studies* 44(3), 429–51.

Alden, C., and D. Large, eds. (2019). *New Directions in Africa–China Studies*. New York: Routledge.

Amin, S. (1972). Underdevelopment and Dependence in Black Africa – Origins and Contemporary Forms. *The Journal of Modern African Studies* 10(4), 503–24.

Amsden, A. (1979). Taiwan's Economic History: A Case of Etatisme and a Challenge to Dependency Theory. *Modern China* 5(3), 341–80.

Anderson, J. L. (1998). The Dictator. *The New Yorker*, October 19.

Apter, D. E., and C. G. Rosberg, eds. (1994). *Political Development and the New Realism in Sub-Saharan Africa*. Charlottesville: University Press of Virginia.

Arrighi, G. (2007). *Adam Smith in Beijing*. London: Verso.

Barrott, L.-D., C. Calderón, and L. Servén (2016). Openness, Specialization, and the External Vulnerability of Developing Countries. Washington DC: World Bank, Policy Research Working Paper 7711.

Baumann, R. (2008). *Integration in Latin America – Trends and Challenges*. Brasilia: ECLAC.

Belassa, B., and F. D. McCarthy (1984). Adjustment Policies in Developing Countries, 1979–83: An Update. Washington, DC: World Bank Staff Working Papers no. 675.

Bernal, R. (2016). *Dragon in the Caribbean: China's Global Re-Dimensioning – Challenges and Opportunities for the Caribbean*, rev. ed. Kingston: Ian Randle Publisher.

Bhattacharya, D. (2007). Moving Out of Aid Dependency: Reflections on LDC Experience. Presentation at Department of Economic and Social Affairs Panel Discussion. New York: United Nations.

Bielschowsky, R. (1998). *Cincuenta Años del Pensamiento de la CEPAL: Textos Seleccionados*. Santiago: ECLAC.

Bielschowsky, R. (2010). *Sesenta Años de la CEPAL: Textos Seleccionados del Decenio 1998–2008*. Santiago: ECLAC.

Bienefeld, M. (1988). Dependency Theory and the Political Economy of Africa's Crisis. *Review of African Political Economy* 43, 68–87.

Birdsall, N., and F. Jasperson, eds. (1997). *Pathways to Growth: Comparing East Asia and Latin America*. Washington, DC: Inter-American Development Bank.

Blattman, C., J. Huang, and J. G. Williamson (2007). Winners and Losers in the Commodity Lottery: The Impact of Terms of Trade Growth and Volatility in the Periphery, 1870–1939. *Journal of Development Economics* 82, 156–79.

Blum, W. (1995). *Killing Hope: US Military and CIA Interventions since World War II*, updated ed. London: Zed Books.

Brautigam, D. (2011). *The Dragon's Gift: The Real Story of China in Africa*. New York: Oxford University Press.

Brett, E. A. (1971). Dependency and Development: Some Problems Involved in the Analysis of Change in Colonial Africa. *Cahiers d'Etudes Africaines* 11 (44), 538–63.

Bruszt, L., and V. Vukov (2018). Governing Market Integration and Development – Lessons from Europe's Eastern and Southern Peripheries. *Studies in Comparative International Development* 53(2), 153–68.

Bulmer-Thomas, V. (2014). *The Economic History of Latin America since Independence*, 3rd ed. New York: Cambridge University Press.

Bulmer-Thomas, V., J. Coatsworth, and R. Cortes Conde, eds. (2006a). *The Cambridge Economic History of Latin America. Vol. I: The Colonial Era and the Short Nineteenth Century*. Cambridge: Cambridge University Press.

Bulmer-Thomas, V., J. Coatsworth, and R. Cortes Conde, eds. (2006b). *The Cambridge Economic History of Latin America. Vol. II: The Long Twentieth Century*. Cambridge: Cambridge University Press.

Campello, D. (2015). *The Politics of Market Discipline in Latin America: Globalization and Democracy*. New York: Cambridge University Press.

Caputo, O., and R. Pizarro (1974). *Dependencia y Relaciones Internacionales*. San Jose: EDUCA.

Cardoso, F. H. (1977). The Consumption of Dependency Theory in the United States. *Latin American Research Review* 12(3), 7–22.

Cardoso, F. H. (2009). New Paths: Globalization in Historical Perspective. *Studies in Comparative International Development* 44 (4), 296–317.

Cardoso, F. H., and E. Faletto (1969). *Dependencia y Desarrollo en América Latina*. Mexico, DF: Siglo XXI.

Cardoso, F. H., and E. Faletto (1979). *Dependency and Development in Latin America*. Berkeley: University of California Press.

Carlsson, J. (1983). Transcending the Blocked Development – The Economic Development of the Ivory Coast. *Acta Sociologica* 26(3/4), 321–27.

Casanova, C., L. Xia, and R. Ferreira (2015). Measuring Latin America's Export Dependency on China, Hong Kong: BBVA Working Paper No. 15/26.

Casey, N., and C. Krauss (2018). It Doesn't Matter if Ecuador Can Afford This Dam. China Still Gets Paid. *New York Times*, December 24.

Castañeda, N. (2017). New Dependency? Economic Links between China and Latin America. *Issues and Studies* 53(1), 1740001-1-33.

Chang, J. (2019). Presentation at panel on "Confronting Latin America's Economic Challenges: What Can the Region Do?" Inter-American Dialogue, Washington DC, July 22.

Chaudhary, M. A. (1988). International Debt and Foreign Dependency: Policy Options for Pakistan. *The Pakistan Development Review* XXVII(4), 829–36.

Chilcote, R., ed. (1982). *Dependency and Marxism: Toward a Resolution of the Debate*. Boulder, CO: Westview Press.

Cline, W. R. (1984). *International Debt: Systemic Risk and Policy Response*. Washington, DC: Institute for International Economics.

Cline, W. R. (1995). *International Debt Reexamined*. Washington, DC: Institute for International Economics.

Denoon, D. B., ed. (2017). *China, the United States, and the Future of Southeast Asia. US–China Relations, Vol. II*. New York: New York University Press.

Devlin, R. (1989). *Debt and Crisis in Latin America: The Supply Side of the Story*. Princeton, NJ: Princeton University Press.

dos Santos, T. (1968). *El Nuevo Carácter de la Dependencia*. Santiago: CESO.

Drake, P. (1989). Debt and Democracy in Latin America, 1920s–1980s. In B. Stallings and R. Kaufman, eds. *Debt and Democracy in Latin America*. Boulder, CO: Westview Press, 39–58.

Drout, B. (2018). Twin Ocean Railroad: A Multilevel Games Analysis of the Chinese Engagement in the Proposed Railroad between Brazil and Argentina. MA Thesis, Schwarzman Scholars Program, Tsinghua University.

Dussel Peters, E. (2018). Monitor of Chinese OFDI in Latin America and the Caribbean in 2018. Red Académica de América Latina y el Caribe sobre China (redalc-china.org).

Dussel Peters, E., and A. C. Armony (2017). *Effects of China on the Quantity and Quality of Jobs in Latin America and the Caribbean*. Geneva: ILO.

Dussel Peters, E., A. C. Armony, and S. Cui, eds. (2018). *Building Development for a New Era: China's Infrastructure Projects in Latin America and the Caribbean*. Pittsburgh: Asian Studies Center, University of Pittsburgh and Red Académica de América Latina y el Caribe sobre China.

Duvall, R. D. (1978). Dependence and Dependencia Theory: Notes toward Precision of Concept and Argument. *International Organization* 32(1), 51–78.

ECLA (1950). *The Economic Development of Latin America and its Principal Problems*. Santiago: ECLA.

ECLAC (2011). *People's Republic of China and Latin America and the Caribbean: Ushering In a New Era in the Economic and Trade Relationship*. Santiago: ECLAC.

ECLAC (2015). *Latin America and the Caribbean and China: Towards a New Era in Economic Cooperation*. Santiago: ECLAC.

ECLAC (2016). *Relaciones Económicas entre América Latina y el Caribe y China: Oportunidades y Desafíos*. Santiago: ECLAC.

ECLAC (2018). *Exploring New Forms of Cooperation between China and Latin America and the Caribbean*. Santiago: ECLAC.

ECLAC (2019a). *Economic Survey of Latin America and the Caribbean, 2019*. Santiago: ECLAC.

ECLAC (2019b). *Social Panorama of Latin America, 2019*. Santiago: ECLAC.

Economy, E. C. (2018). *The Third Revolution: Xi Jinping and the New Chinese State*. New York: Oxford University Press.

Eisenman, J., and E. Heginbotham, eds. (2018). *China Steps Out: Beijing's Major Power Engagement with the Developing World*. New York: Routledge.

Ellis, R. E. (2009). *China in Latin America: The Whats and Wherefores*. Boulder, CO: Lynne Rienner.

Ellis, R. E. (2013). *The Strategic Dimension of Chinese Engagement with Latin America*. Perry Paper Series No. 1. Washington, DC: William J. Perry Center for Hemispheric Defense Studies.

Ellis, R. E. (2018). The Impact of China on the Latin American Security Environment. *Revista da Escola de Guerra Naval* 24(2), 456–62.

Elten, H. (2018). Chinese Infrastructure Investment in Cambodia: Implications and Consequences. MA Thesis, Schwarzman Scholars Program, Tsinghua University.

Evans, P. (1979). *Dependent Development: The Alliance of Multinational, State, and Local Capital in Brazil*. Princeton, NJ: Princeton University Press.

Feng, Z., and J. Huang (2014). China's Strategic Partnership Diplomacy: Engaging with a Changing World. Madrid: FRIDE, European Strategic Partnership Observatory Working Paper 8.

Ferchen, M., A. García-Herrero, and M. Nigrinis (2013). Evaluating Latin American Commodity Dependence on China. Hong Kong: BBVA Economic Research Department Working Paper 1305.

Frank, A. G. (1967). *Capitalism and Underdevelopment in Latin America: Historical Studies of Chile and Brazil*. New York: Monthly Review Press.

French, H. (2017). *Everything under the Heavens: How the Past Helps Shape China's Push for Global Power*. New York: Knopf.

Frieden, J. (1981). Third World Indebted Industrialization: International Finance and State Capitalism in Mexico, Brazil, Algeria, and South Korea. *International Organization* 35(3): 407–31.

Fukuyama, F. (1992). *The End of History and the Last Man*. New York: The Free Press.

Gallagher, K. P. (2016). *The China Triangle: Latin America's China Boom and the Fate of the Washington Consensus*. New York: Oxford University Press.

Gallagher, K. P., and R. Porzecanski (2010). *The Dragon in the Room: China and the Future of Latin American Industrialization*. Stanford, CA: Stanford University Press.

Gallagher, K., A. Irwin, and K. Koleski (2012). *The New Banks in Town: Chinese Finance in Latin America*. Washington, DC: The Interamerican Dialogue.

Gereffi, G. (1989). Rethinking Development Theory: Insights from East Asia and Latin America. *Sociological Forum* 4(4), 505–32.

Gereffi, G., and D. L. Wyman, eds. (1990). *Manufacturing Miracles: Patterns of Development in Latin America and East Asia*. Princeton, NJ: Princeton University Press.

Goh, E., ed. (2016). *Rising China's Influence in Developing Asia*. New York: Oxford University Press.

González, F. E. (2008). Latin America in the Economic Equation – Winners and Losers: What Can the Losers Do? In R. Roett and G. Paz, eds. *China's Expansion into the Western Hemisphere: Implications for Latin America and the United States*. Washington, DC: The Brookings Institution Press, 148–69.

Griffith-Jones, S., ed. (1988). *Managing World Debt*. London: Harvester Wheatsheaf.

Guo, J. (2015). History and Changes of Shougang Hierro Peru. *Journal of International Studies* 36(1), 51–73.

Gurrola, G. (2018). China–Latin America Arms Sales: Antagonizing the United States in the Western Hemisphere? *Military Review*, July–August.

Haggard, S. (1986). The Newly Industrializing Countries in the International System. *World Politics* 38(2), 343–70.

Haggard, S. (1990). *Pathways from the Periphery: The Politics of Growth in the Newly Industrializing Countries*. Ithaca, NY: Cornell University Press.

Haggard, S. (2018). *Developmental States*. New York: Cambridge University Press.

Harvey, D. (2005). *A Brief History of Neoliberalism*. New York: Oxford University Press.

Hassan, M.D. (2011). Foreign Aid Dependency of Bangladesh: An Evaluation. *The Chittagong University Journal of Business Administration* 26, 281–94.

Heginbotham, E. (2018). China's Strategy in Southeast Asia. In J. Eisenman and E. Heginbotham, eds. *China Steps Out: Beijing's Major Power Engagement with the Developing World.* New York: Routledge.

Higgott, R. (1980). Structural Dependence and Decolonization in a West African Land-Locked State: Niger. *Review of African Political Economy* 17, 43–58.

Horn, S., C. Reinhart, and C. Trebesch (2019). China's Overseas Lending. Kiel: Kiel Institute for the World Economy Working Paper 2132.

IMF. *Direction of Trade Statistics* (data.imf.org).

Inter-American Development Bank (1999). *Facing Up to Inequality in Latin America. Economic and Social Progress in Latin America, 1998–99 Report.* Washington, DC: IDB.

Inter-American Development Bank (2010). *Ten Years after the Take-Off: Taking Stock of China-Latin America and the Caribbean Economic Relations.* Washington, DC: Inter-American Development Bank.

Inter-American Development Bank (2014). *LAC Investment in China: A New Chapter in Latin America and the Caribbean–China Relations.* Washington, DC: Inter-American Development Bank.

Jackman, R. W. (1982). Dependence on Foreign Investment and Economic Growth in the Third World. *World Politics* 34(2), 175–96.

Jenkins, R. (2012). Latin America and China – A New Dependency? *Third World Quarterly* 33(7), 1337–58.

Jenkins, R. (2019). *How China Is Reshaping the Global Economy: Development Impacts in Africa and Latin America.* New York: Oxford University Press.

Kahler, M. (1990). Orthodoxy and its Alternatives: Explaining Approaches to Stabilization and Adjustment. In J. M. Nelson, ed., *Economic Crisis and Policy Choice: The Politics of Adjustment in the Third World.* Princeton, NJ: Princeton University Press.

Kahn, A. A., and M. Z. Asghar (2015). The Study of Aid Dependency and External Debt on Pakistan's Economy. *Journal of Poverty, Investment and Development* 8, 156–65.

Kaplan, S. B. (2016). Banking Unconditionally: The Political Economy of Chinese Finance in Latin America. *Review of International Political Economy* 23(4), 643–76.

Kaplan, S. B. (forthcoming). *The Rise of Patient Capital: The Political Economy of Chinese Global Finance in Latin America.* New York: Cambridge University Press.

Kaplan, S. B., and M. Penfold (2019). *China–Venezuela Economic Relations: Hedging Venezuelan Bets with Chinese Characteristics.* Washington, DC: Woodrow Wilson Center.

Kaufman, R. R., H. I. Chernotsky, and D. S. Geller (1975). A Preliminary Test of the Theory of Dependency. *Comparative Politics* 7(3), 303–30.

Kindiki, M. M. (2014). Dependency in International Regimes: The Case of the Apparel Industry in Sub-Saharan Africa. *Review of African Political Economy* 41(142), 594–608.

Kinzer, S. (2006). *Overthrow: America's Century of Regime Change from Hawaii to Iraq*. New York: Times Books.

Kohli, A. (2004). *State-Directed Development: Political Power and Industrialization in the Global Periphery*. New York: Cambridge University Press.

Koleski, K., and A. Blivas (2018). China's Engagement with Latin America and the Caribbean. US–China Economic and Security Review Commission, Staff Research Report.

Krugman, P. (1991). *Geography and Trade*. Cambridge, MA: MIT Press.

Kurlantzick, J. (2008). *Charm Offensive: How China's Soft Power Is Transforming the World*. New Haven, CT: Yale University Press.

LaFeber, W. (1989). *The American Age: United States Foreign Policy at Home and Abroad since 1750*. New York: W. W. Norton.

Lardy, N. R. (2002). *Integrating China into the Global Economy*. Washington, DC: The Brookings Institution Press.

Leaf, P. J. (2014). China's Charm Offensive: A Temporary, Tactical Change. *The Diplomat*, December 17.

Levitsky, S., and K. M. Roberts, eds. (2011). *The Resurgence of the Latin American Left*. Baltimore: Johns Hopkins University Press.

Leys, C. (1975). *Underdevelopment in Kenya: The Political Economy of Neo-Colonialism 1964–71*. London: Heinemann.

Li, C., and C. Yang (2018). *Forget Stanford, Tsinghua Beckons*. Washington, DC: The Brookings Institution.

Lin, J. Y., and V. Treichel (2012). Learning from China's Rise to Escape the Middle-Income Trap: A New Structural Economics Approach to Latin America. Washington, DC: World Bank Policy Research Paper No. 6165.

Londono, E. (2018). From a Space Station in Argentina, China Expands its Reach in Latin America. *New York Times*, July 28.

Look Lai, W. (2010). Asian Diasporas and Tropical Migration in the Age of Empire: A Comparative Overview. In W. Look Lai and C. B. Tan, eds. *The Chinese in Latin America and the Caribbean*. Leiden: Koninklijke Brill NV.

López-Calva, L. F., and N. Lustig, eds. (2010). *Declining Inequality in Latin America: A Decade of Progress?* Washington, DC: The Brookings Institution and UNDP.

Luksic, T. (2019). Global Value Chain Upgrading Strategies and Policy Implications: An Evaluation of the Lithium Mining Industry in Chile. MA Thesis, Schwarzman Scholars Program, Tsinghua University.

Maddison, A. (2007). *Contours of the World Economy 1–2030AD: Essays in Macro-Economic History.* Oxford: Oxford University Press.

Marini, R. M. (1972). Dialéctica de la Dependencia: La Economía Exportadora. *Sociedad y Desarrollo* 1, 5–31.

Marshall, J., J. L. Mardones, and I. Marshall (1983). IMF Conditionality: The Experience of Argentina, Brazil, and Chile. In J. Williamson, ed. *IMF Conditionality.* Washington, DC: Institute for International Economics.

McCartney, M. (2011). Pakistan, Growth, Dependency, and Crisis. *Lahore Journal of Economics* 16, 71–94.

McGowan, P. (1976). Economic Dependence and Economic Performance in Black Africa. *Journal of Modern African Studies* 14(1), 25–40.

McGowan, P., and D. L. Smith (1978). Economic Dependency in Black Africa: The Analysis of Competing Theories. *International Organization* 32(1), 179–235.

McPherson, A. (2016). *A Short History of U.S. Interventions in Latin America and the Caribbean.* New York: Wiley Blackwell.

Messina, J., and J. Silva (2017). *Wage Inequality in Latin America: Understanding the Past to Prepare for the Future.* Washington, DC: World Bank.

Moss, T. J., G. P. Gelander, and N. van de Walle (2005). An Aid-Institutions Paradox? A Review Essay on Aid Dependency and State Building in Sub-Saharan Africa. Washington, DC: Center for Global Development Working Paper 74.

Munck, R. (1984). *The Politics of Dependency in the Third World.* London: Zed Books.

Myers, M. (2018). *China's Transport Infrastructure in LAC: Five Things to Know.* Washington, DC: Inter-American Dialogue.

Myers, M., and K. Gallagher (2016). *Chinese Finance to LAC in 2016.* Washington, DC: Inter-American Dialogue.

Myers, M., and K. Gallagher (2017). *Down but not Out: Chinese Development Finance in LAC, 2017.* Washington, DC: Inter-American Dialogue.

National Endowment for Democracy (2017). *Sharp Power: Rising Authoritarian Influence.* Washington, DC: NED.

Naughton, B. (2006). *The Chinese Economy: Transitions and Growth.* Cambridge, MA: MIT Press.

Naughton, B. (2018). *The Chinese Economy: Adaptation and Growth*, 2nd ed. Cambridge, MA: MIT Press.

Needham, J. (1954). *Science and Civilization in China. Vol. I: Introductory Orientations*. Cambridge: Cambridge University Press.

Nye, J. S. (2004). *Soft Power: The Means to Success in World Politics*. New York: Public Affairs.

Ocampo, J. A., B. Stallings, I. Bustillo, H. Velloso, and R. Frenkel. (2014). *La crisis latinoamericana de la deuda desde la perspectiva histórica*. Santiago: ECLAC.

OECD/ECLAC/CAF (2015). *Latin American Economic Outlook 2016: Towards a New Partnership with China*. Paris: OECD.

Okolo, A. (1983). Dependency in Africa: Stages of African Political Economy. *Alternatives* 9(2), 229–47.

Ortiz, J. (2012). Deja Vu: Latin America and Its New Trade Dependency . . . This Time with China. *Latin American Research Review* 47(3), 175–90.

Packenham, R. (1982). Plus Ca Change . . . The English Edition of Cardoso and Faletto's Dependencia y Desarrollo en América Latina. *Latin American Research Review* 17(1), 131–51.

Palma, G. (1978). Dependency: A Formal Theory of Underdevelopment or a Methodology for the Analysis of Concrete Situations of Underdevelopment. *World Development* 6(7–8), 881–924.

Parajon, C. (2019). The Impact on Central America of the 2008–2016 Diplomatic Truce between Chinese Mainland and Taiwan. MA Thesis, Schwarzman Scholars Program, Tsinghua University.

Patey, L. (2017). China Made Mauricio Macri an Offer He Couldn't Refuse. *Foreign Policy*, January 24.

Pei, M. (2018). The Limits of China's Charm Offensive. *Project Syndicate*, November 19.

People's Republic of China, Ministry of Foreign Affairs (2008). *China's Policy Paper on Latin America and the Caribbean*. Beijing: MOFA.

People's Republic of China, Ministry of Foreign Affairs (2014). *Xi Jinping Attends China–Latin America and the Caribbean Summit and Delivers Keynote Speech*. Beijing: MOFA.

People's Republic of China, Ministry of Foreign Affairs (2016). *China's Policy Paper on Latin America and the Caribbean*. Beijing: MOFA.

Perrotti, D. (2015). The People's Republic of China and Latin America: The Impact of Chinese Economic Growth on Latin American Exports. *CEPAL Review* 116: 47–59.

Piccone, T. (2016). *The Geopolitics of China's Rise in Latin America*. Washington, DC: The Brookings Institution.

Przeworski, A. (1990). What We Don't Know about Capitalism, Socialism, and Democracy. Chicago: University of Chicago East–West System Transition Working Paper, No. 1.

Ray, R., K. Gallagher, A. López, and C. Sanborn, eds. (2017). *China and Sustainable Development in Latin America: The Social and Environmental Dimension*. New York: Anthem Press.

Reed, J. (2019). Cambodian Leader Denies Plan to Host Chinese Military Base. *Financial Times*, July 22.

Remmer, K. (1990). Democracy and Economic Crisis. In D. Felix, ed. *Debt and Transformation? Prospects for Latin America's Economic Revival*. New York: M. E. Sharpe.

Rhodes, W. R. (2011). *Banker to the World: Leadership Lessons from the Front Lines of Global Finance*. New York: McGraw-Hill.

Rocha, F. F., and R. Bielschowsky (2018). La Búsqueda de China de Recursos Naturales en América Latina. *Revista CEPAL* 126, 9–29.

Rostow, W. W. (1960). *The Economic Stages of Growth: A Non-Communist Manifesto*. Cambridge: Cambridge University Press.

Schwartz, H. (2007). Dependency or Institutions? Economic Geography, Causal Mechanisms, and Logic in the Understanding of Development. *Studies in Comparative International Development* 42(1–2), 115–35.

Shepard, W. (2017). China's Seaport Shopping Spree: What China Is Winning by Buying Up the World's Ports. *Forbes*, September 17.

Sheppard, E. (2010). Adam Smith in Beijing: Lineages of the Twenty-first Century. *Economic Geography* 86(1), 99–101.

Shinn, D. H., and J. Eisenman (2012). *China and Africa: A Century of Engagement*. Philadelphia: University of Pennsylvania Press.

Sobhan, R. (1996). *Aid Dependence and Donor Policy: The Case of Tanzania with Lessons from Bangladesh's Experience*. Dhaka: University Press Ltd.

Solis, M., B. Stallings, and S. Katada, eds. (2009). *Competitive Regionalism: FTA Diffusion in the Pacific Rim*. New York: Palgrave/Macmillan.

Solow, R. M. (1956). A Contribution to the Theory of Economic Growth. *The Quarterly Journal of Economics* 70(1), 65–94.

Spring, J. (2018). Bolsonaro's Anti-China Rants Have Beijing Nervous about Brazil. *Reuters*, October 25.

Stallings, B. (1972). *Economic Dependency in Africa and Latin America*. Beverly Hills, CA: Sage Publications.

Stallings, B. (1987). *Banker to the Third World: US Portfolio Investment in Latin America, 1900–1986*. Berkeley, CA: University of California Press.

Stallings, B. (1992). International Influence on Economic Policy: Debt, Stabilization, and Structural Reform. In S. Haggard and R. Kaufman, eds. *The Politics of Economic Adjustment: International Constraints, Distributive Politics, and the State*. Princeton, NJ: Princeton University Press.

Stallings, B. (2008). The US-China-Latin America Triangle: Implications for the Future. In R. Roett and G. Paz, eds. *China's Expansion into the Western Hemisphere: Implications for Latin America and the United States.* Washington, DC: The Brookings Institution Press, 239–59.

Stallings, B. (2009). Chile: A Pioneer in Trade Policy. In M. Solis, B. Stallings, and S. Katada, eds. *Competitive Regionalism: FTA Diffusion in the Pacific Rim.* New York: Palgrave/Macmillan, 118–38.

Stallings, B. (2017). Chinese Foreign Aid to Latin America: Trying to Win Friends and Influence People. In M. Myers and C. Wise, eds. *The Political Economy of China-Latin American Relations in the New Millennium.* New York: Routledge, 69–91.

Stallings, B. (2018). China and its Neighbors: Aid and Investment in East Asia. Presentation at 11th Annual Conference on China. Washington, DC: George Washington University, Institute for International Economic Policy.

Stallings, B., and E. M. Kim (2017). *Promoting Development: The Political Economy of East Asian Foreign Aid.* New York: Palgrave Macmillan.

Stallings, B., and W. Peres (2000). *Growth, Employment, and Equity: The Impact of the Economic Reforms in Latin America and the Caribbean.* Washington, DC: The Brookings Institution and ECLAC.

Stromseth, J. (2019). The Testing Ground: China's Rising Influence in Southeast Asia and Regional Responses. Washington DC: The Brookings Institution, Global China Program.

Swan, T. (1956). Economic Growth and Capital Accumulation. *Economic Record* 32(63), 334–61.

Swine, M. D., and M. T. Fravel (2011). China's Assertive Behavior, Part Two: The Maritime Periphery. *China's Leadership Monitor* 35, 1–29.

Taylor, I. (2014). *Africa Rising? BRICS – Diversifying Dependency.* Melton: James Currey.

Thorp, R. (1998). *Progress, Poverty and Exclusion: An Economic History of Latin America in the 20th Century.* Washington, DC: Interamerican Development Bank.

Valenzuela, J. S., and A. Valenzuela (1978). Modernization and Dependency: Alternative Perspectives to the Study of Latin American Underdevelopment. *Comparative Politics* 10(4), 535–57.

Vengroff, R. (1977). Dependency and Underdevelopment in Black Africa: An Empirical Test. *The Journal of Modern African Studies* 15(4), 613–30.

von Thunen, J. H. (1966). *Von Thunen's Isolated State: An English Edition.* Oxford: Pergamon Press.

Wallerstein, I. (1974). *The Modern World-System: Capitalist Agriculture and the Origins of the European World Economy in the Sixteenth Century.* New York: Academic Press.

Wallerstein, I. (1976). Semi-Peripheral Countries and the Contemporary World Crisis. *Theory and Society* 3(4), 461–83.

Walz, J. (2018). Latin American Public Opinion on China: Drivers and Implications. MA Thesis, Schwarzman Scholars Program, Tsinghua University.

Warren, B. (1980). *Imperialism: Pioneer of Capitalism.* London: New Left Books.

Williamson, J., ed. (1990). *Latin American Adjustment: How Much Has Happened?* Washington, DC: Institute for International Economics.

Wise, C. (2016). Playing Both Sides of the Pacific: Latin America's Free Trade Agreements (FTAs) with China. *Pacific Affairs* 89(1), 75–101.

Wise, C. (2020). *Dragonomics: The Rise of China in Latin America.* New Haven, CT: Yale University Press.

World Bank (2011). *Latin America and the Caribbean's Long-Term Growth: Made in China?* Washington, DC: World Bank.

World Bank. *World Development Indicators* (wdi.worldbank.org).

Xu, Y. (2017). *China's Strategic Partnerships in Latin America: Case Studies of China's Oil Diplomacy in Argentina, Brazil, Mexico, and Venezuela.* Lanham, MD: Lexington Books.

Yates, D. A. (1996). *The Rentier State in Africa: Oil Rent Dependency and Neocolonialism in the Republic of Gabon.* Trenton, NJ: Africa World Press.

Zartman, I. W. (1976). Europe and Africa: Decolonization or Dependency? *Foreign Affairs* 54(2), 325–43.

Zhang, J. (2019). *Belt and Road in Latin America: A Regional Game Changer?* Washington DC: The Atlantic Council.

Cambridge Elements ☰

Elements in Politics and Society in Latin America

Maria Victoria Murillo

Columbia University

Maria Victoria Murillo is Professor of Political Science and International Affairs at Columbia University. She is the author of *Political Competition, Partisanship, and Policymaking in the Reform of Latin American Public Utilities* (Cambridge, 2009). She is also editor of *Carreras Magisteriales, Desempeño Educativo y Sindicatos de Maestros en América Latina* (2003), and co-editor of *Argentine Democracy: the Politics of Institutional Weakness* (2005). She has published in edited volumes as well as in the *American Journal of Political Science, World Politics, Comparative Political Studies* among others.

Juan Pablo Luna

The Pontifical Catholic University of Chile

Juan Pablo Luna is Professor in the Department of Political Science at The Pontifical Catholic University of Chile. He is the author of *Segmented Representation. Political Party Strategies in Unequal Democracies*, and has co-authored *Latin American Party Systems* (Cambridge, 2010). His work on political representation, state capacity, and organized crime has appeared in *Comparative Political Studies, Revista de Ciencia Política*, the *Journal of Latin American Studies, Latin American Politics and Society, Studies in Comparative International Development* among others.

Tulia G. Falleti

University of Pennsylvania

Tulia G. Falleti is the Class of 1965 Term Associate Professor of Political Science, Director of the Latin American and Latino Studies Program, and Senior Fellow of the Leonard Davis Institute for Health Economics at the University of Pennsylvania. She is the author of the award-winning *Decentralization and Subnational Politics in Latin America* (Cambridge, 2010). She is co-editor of *The Oxford Handbook of Historical Institutionalism*, among other edited books. Her articles have appeared in many edited volumes and journals such as the *American Political Science Review* and *Comparative Political Studies*.

Andrew Schrank

Brown University

Andrew Schrank is the Olive C. Watson Professor of Sociology and International & Public Affairs at Brown University. His articles on business, labor, and the state in Latin America have appeared in the *American Journal of Sociology, Comparative Politics, Comparative Political Studies, Latin American Politics & Society, Social Forces*, and *World Development*, among other journals, and his co-authored book, *Root-Cause Regulation: Labor Inspection in Europe and the Americas*, is out soon.

About the Series

Latin American politics and society are at a crossroads, simultaneously confronting serious challenges and remarkable opportunities that are likely to be shaped by formal institutions and informal practices alike. The new Politics and Society in Latin America Cambridge Elements series will offer multidisciplinary and methodologically pluralist contributions on the most important topics and problems confronted by the region.